Out of the Blue

VICTORIA FALLS

Out of the Blue

ESSAYS ON BOOKS
ART AND TRAVEL

Written and
Illustrated by

CHESTER WOODWARD

Essay Index Reprint Series

BOOKS FOR LIBRARIES PRESS
FREEPORT, NEW YORK

First Published 1938
Reprinted 1969

STANDARD BOOK NUMBER:
8369-1239-X

LIBRARY OF CONGRESS CATALOG CARD NUMBER:
75-90697

PRINTED IN THE UNITED STATES OF AMERICA

1503974

Table of Contents

Illustrations

Introductory Note

By Douglas C. McMurtrie

*H*ow few successful American business men gain profit and enjoyment from the potential leisure earned by their accomplishments! The majority go to their graves direct from the confining routine of their office, without ever taking time out to do some of the things they dimly hoped to do "when opportunity offered."

Many others who do retire are at a loss to put their available time to interesting and enjoyable use because they had not previously built up, slowly and naturally, some leisure-time interest which might properly grow into a full-time hobby. So they are reduced to the two standard off-hours activities for American males: golf and bridge.

The man with non-commercial enthusiasms of his individual choosing is becoming more and more the exception. More's the pity that this is the case, for such personal enthusiasms frequently redound to the great advantage of the community. To such enthusiasms must be credited many of the more important collections of books and art in libraries and museums throughout the land and to them we must ascribe responsibility for the erection and endowment of many institutions rendering valuable public service.

It is the principal merit of the present volume that it records three non-commercial enthusiasms of an American business man: hobbies ridden in the years both before and after retirement. Because these essays tell of the precious interest of a man universally regarded as one of Topeka's first citizens, I encouraged Chester Woodward to write this manuscript and to put into it more personal and intimate references than I think he was inclined to. And in recent months, I have even "ragged" him a bit to complete the copy and prepare the illustrations.

Chester Woodward comes of pioneer Kansas stock. His father, who was a Pennsylvania Quaker, came to Kansas in 1855, to contribute his bit toward making that territory a free state. A drug store, which he established at Lawrence, grew into a large wholesale drug business in Kansas City, Missouri. In spite of this frontier environment, he developed a keen interest in art and literature, and built up one of the first art collections west of the Mississippi. The father also wrote and published a volume of poems and essays, which were commended by such men as James Russell Lowell, John G. Whittier, and Oliver Wendell Holmes. We see, therefore, that our present author came by, quite honestly and naturally, an interest in books and art.

After graduating from the University of Kansas, Chester Woodward began his career as a pharmacist. He tells me there was no "hours and wages" act in force at that time, for he often tended store from six in the morning until eleven at night, and then slept in quarters over the store, so that he could answer night calls.

With savings accumulated during this easy employment, he entered the farm loan business, and from this became engaged in general banking. For many years he was vice-president of a large national bank and trust company and has for twenty

14

years been president of the Topeka Morris Plan Company. So much for business.

Outside of business, Chester Woodward's experience has been similarly rich and varied. For ten years member of the local Board of Education, he was its president for two years during which an active building program was undertaken. His presidency for many years of the Topeka Library Board and vice-presidency of the Art Guild of Topeka give further evidence of his interest in books and art as community assets. Mr. Woodward has also taken an active interest in civic art and architecture and in city planning, as will appear from the chapter on art in this volume.

A further active interest in the cause of education is evidenced by Mr. Woodward's membership on the board of trustees of Washburn College and the advisory board of Yenching University in China. Last year he was national president of the Alumni Association of the University of Kansas. During the World War our author served at Washington as national associate director of Canteen Service.

In the loam of this experience in business and community service have been nurtured the personal enthusiasms in travel, art, and books discussed informally in the following essays. And I should add that there is a fourth enthusiasm, not named on the title page, which integrates admirably with these three. I refer to photography, for Chester Woodward has become so proficient in the use of the camera as to have taken prizes for prints entered in international competition. He took the photographs which illustrate this volume.

It is my hope that many readers will share in Chester Woodward's enthusiasms by reading the pages which follow and, mayhap, be thereby inspired to find, enjoy, and profit from some individually-chosen enthusiasms of their own.

Douglas C. McMurtrie

November 24, 1938

"Let us probe the silent spaces,
Let us seek what luck betides us,
Let us journey to a lovely land I know.
There's a whisper on the night wind,
There's a star agleam to guide us,
And the wild is calling, calling — let us go."

I

South African Adventure

*W*HEN I WAS A BOY I lived in the shadow of a great university. My particular hero, in those days, was an advanced student of natural history. He was learning taxidermy and he used to take me to the laboratory where I watched him mount the bones of "Ethan Allen," a famous racehorse, and stuff the hide of old "Comanche," General Custer's renowned war horse. Little did I realize then that William Harvey Brown was before many years to become an empire builder, a pioneer of the Dark Continent, South Africa, along with Cecil Rhodes, in that vast wilderness of Rhodesia he was later to explore. But he went away to Africa and stayed for years and when he came back he was more my hero than ever. He would tell me stories of his life and adventures in this wild and interesting country for hours, stories of the bush, the natives and the wild animals. Stories of the gold and diamond mines, of Cecil Rhodes, whose intimate friend he became and a thousand other things that would interest a boy. William Harvey Brown was to return to South Africa again and again, and grow with that great country. He became a member of the Rhodesian parliament. He was an explorer, a soldier and a statesman. On one of his trips back home he wrote a book *On the South African Frontier,* one of the most interesting stories of adventure in South Africa ever written. I have read and reread the copy he gave me, with the keenest interest.

As I look back now, I know Will Brown and his book started a longing in my heart to see, some day, the country he loved so much, a longing that was destined to be gratified only after many years of waiting.

And now that I have been there, and travelled over that fascinating country and returned from the thirty-thousand-mile journey, I want to tell of some of the things I did, and some of the things I saw, as well as a few of my personal impressions of the country.

In the first place, how little we know of this vast and intensely interesting part of the globe! Most of us know, probably, from our geography and history days, that it is a great place for wild animals, diamonds and gold; that Cecil Rhodes founded there a great empire; that there was a Boer war, with President Kruger and the Boers on one side, and the English on the other; and that the English won this war. Now throw in the names of three cities, Capetown, Kimberley and Johannesburg, and that is about all the average man knows off-hand about South Africa.

But before we go down there, let us very briefly rehearse the history of what is about the most enchanting country I know. A long time ago South Africa was considered merely as an obstacle in the way of shortening the trade route from Europe to India; indeed, it was supposed that the Indian Ocean was landlocked. It was not until five years after Columbus had discovered America, that a Portuguese navigator, Bartholomeu Dias, sailing south, doubled the Cape of Good Hope and went about half way up the east side of the continent before he gave up and started for home, discouraged. Ten years later, Vasco da Gama, another Portuguese, again doubled the Cape, sailed on and reached India. We thus see that the discovery of South Africa was merely incidental. That was four and a half centuries ago; since then the tides of empire have risen and fallen a great many times.

South Africa was originally inhabited by men of the Stone Age, and their remains are still to be found all over the country. They were followed by the Bushmen, who are still to be seen there and are ethnologically the oldest of all surviving races. The Bushman was almost exterminated by the Hottentot who was in turn nearly wiped out by the Bantu. The Bushman and the Hottentot were small yellow men; but the Bantu, who came down from Central Africa, was a black man. Intensely black. The Bantu race spread all over the country, divided and subdivided, and its descendants form most of the black or native tribes found all over southern Africa today. At present, there are only about ten million inhabitants in all South Africa, eight million of whom are natives, and the other two million whites of various nationalities.

During the intervening years, since the discovery of South Africa by the white man, have come the British, the Dutch, the Huguenots and Malays, and, on the eastern coast, a considerable number of East Indians. It has not been a peaceful development during this long period, at any time. Troublous times are inevitable when a white race comes in and subjugates or drives out the native inhabitants of a country. This was especially true when the Dutch pioneer farmers or voortrekkers began to colonize on the west coast and to push eastward in search of the rich farm lands. They were followed by the English, whose disputes with the Boers were supposed to have been settled by the Boer war at the turn of the century. The English won the war; and South Africa today is a British colony; but the Boers are at the present time in predominance in Parliament and the strong antagonistic feeling between the two elements still exists.

Today the Union of South Africa consists of four states: Cape Colony, Orange Free State, the Transvaal and Natal. Each Province is locally governed by an administrator and an executive committee. The central government has, at its head, a Governor-General appointed by the King; an executive council which corresponds to our cabinet; a Senate, partly appointive and partly elective; and a House of Assembly, the number of whose members is based on the adult white population of each of the Provinces.

In addition to the Provinces, there are three territories or Protectorates: Basutoland, Bechuanaland and Swaziland, vast tracts of land set aside for the use of natives much as was our old Indian Territory, governed directly by the crown through a high commissioner and a native council. Then there are the two Rhodesias. North Rhodesia is under direct control of the crown, while South Rhodesia has its own responsible government. This leaves one more large territory, South West Africa, which was formerly German territory but is now governed, under a mandate of the Versailles Treaty, by England.

This, in a nut-shell, is an outline of the country we are going to visit. South Africa has so far been neglected by American travellers, and probably always will be except by big game hunters who go there only for that purpose and a few others who go for business reasons. It is so far away, so off the beaten path of world travellers, that our little party of eight was the only American tourist group in all South Africa last winter as far as I know. Yet so many people have said to me since I returned, "That is the one country on this earth I want to visit most; it seems so mysterious, so romantic and adventuresome. Tell me about it!"— that I have decided to give them some first hand information and personal experiences gathered in my short three months of African travel.

There is no direct route from our country to South Africa except perhaps an occasional freight boat, which would be a delightful way to go if one had the time and enjoyed long ocean voyages. But we chose to go first to England, and to spend a few days there before trans-shipping to the Union Castle line, which is the only passenger service between England and Cape-town. The first leg of the journey, from New York to South-ampton, seems almost like commuting to me now. It was my ninth crossing, but the Atlantic in January is always turbulent, and when great seas began to smash in the "Berengaria's" port-holes, it was no joke. The shores of old England looked mighty good to us after six days of such stormy weather. We had three days in London, and let me say here, please, please don't go to England in winter.

LONDON IN JANUARY
(Notes From My Diary)

If you have been to London, you no doubt have very pleasant recollections of it. Your visit was probably in the summer time, when the weather was delightful. I have been coming here for almost forty years and with the exception of one visit, in March, when I almost froze to death, I have experienced fine weather. I have never seen a real London fog. But fortunately one soon forgets the unpleasant things of travel; and I had always wanted to be in good old England at Christmas time, especially after a good dose of Dickens' *Christmas Carol,* or some other author's tales of Merrie England in winter. Now all that desire is gone forever—at least until London comes to efficient central heating plants, which will never be in our time. The English don't like them. It certainly is no place for a white man in cold weather, especially an American white man. I have been in London now for three days; it is the middle of January; and I have not been warm, nor found a warm spot, one minute of the time except when I am in bed. Today, as I sat in an office, I noticed a ther-mometer. It read fifty-six degrees and, as I shivered and shook, I asked the Englishman to whom I was talking, how they stood

21

it so cold. He looked at me rather contemptuously and replied, "How in the world do you stand it at seventy degrees in America?" Hotels, theaters, stores, art galleries — everywhere you go it is the same icebox temperature, and you are thoroughly miserable. No wonder Pepys said so often "and so to bed." It is the only place in which you can be comfortably warm in England in January!

London is changing and changing rapidly. It is a fascinating game, finding the bits that are left of the past; but they are becoming few and far between. Some years ago people began moving out into the suburban districts in order to get away from the dirt and noise of downtown London. Besides, with the old type of low buildings, it was an economic necessity. Now they are moving back again to live in modern apartment buildings. These new apartments rival those of New York and are springing up everywhere, especially on all sides of the parks and squares. Here, along Hyde Park, where we are staying, are at least a dozen new apartment buildings in course of construction; and so it goes all over the park districts of London.

Another thing, the noise is gone. London is now the quietest big city in the world. That is one of the characteristics of the English which I admire. They hate noise, especially noisy voices, a thing in which we Americans specialize. You never hear an automobile horn, nor the raucous street cries of the newsboy. Street traffic here can be handled without blowing a siren; and the newsboy simply hangs a large sign from his neck instead of yelling his wares. There isn't even the rumble and roar of a great city. At night it is so quiet that you might think you were in the country, instead of in the heart of the largest city in the world. It is cleaner, it is quieter than of old — but it is so cold!

I thought prices were high in New York, but they don't compare with those of London, especially in the cost of food and drink. A modest breakfast is a dollar and a quarter; lunch, a dollar seventy-five; and dinner, two dollars and a half, drinks not included. The drinks are much higher than with us and they used to be so cheap! I wonder if this isn't because of the terrific tax to help pay for the war? The "Pubs" seem to be gone. They used to be the poor man's club. Probably they have gone on account of the high price of alcoholic beverages, which is possibly just as well, as you see no drunkenness now where formerly there was so much. I have not seen a beggar as yet, although New York seemed to be full of them even with our "managed prosperity."

But the London people do not change. They are the same kindly, polite folk they have always been. Never too hurried to stop and chat, to direct you on your way, or to be helpful in any way possible. The shop-keeper is never too busy, no matter whether you have bought anything or not, to accompany you to the door and bid you a cheery goodbye. That has always been one of the charms of this great city. Somehow you always feel at home here and among your own people.

In the three days we have been here, the weather has been mostly cloudy and gloomy. It has rained a great deal and the cold has been most penetrating and disagreeable; but the elevator boy, tonight, in trying to be pleasant and cordial remarked, "Well you cawn't say we haven't given you good weather while you were here, can you?" Such are the English people. They have a strong climate, which would seem to develop a strong race. You can't down them; and it is this spirit that is bringing them out of the world's greatest depression ahead of all the other countries. England, with her far flung colonies and her proximity to the boiling political pot of Europe, has more problems than any other country; but the indomitable spirit of William the Conqueror and of all the other strong characters in her national history lives on.

So now let us sail away from this stern climate and rugged shores for a few months and come back when nature smiles again in April.

23

Sailing day again, back to Southampton by boat train and aboard the good ship "Windsor Castle" which was to take us on the long trip to Capetown, nearly six thousand miles away, with Madeira the only port of call and shore leave there of only a few hours. We had been there twenty-five years ago and it looked just the same as it did then. Madeira is certainly one of the jewel islands of the South Atlantic, and I look forward to a longer visit on the return trip.

The long sea voyage down the west coast of Africa is almost certain to be a pleasant one. Once you are through the English Channel and have crossed the Bay of Biscay, so apt to be one of the roughest bodies of water in the world, your troubles are over, as far as storms are concerned, until you reach the Cape. Shortly after leaving Madeira we passed through the Canary Islands; and that was the last land we saw until the headlands back of Capetown were sighted. Day after day we steamed through the quiet tropic waters of the Atlantic, with blue skies above and the intensely blue ocean around us. Hardly another ship was sighted the whole two weeks; and it was a peaceful, quiet and restful trip.

On such a long sea voyage, on a comparatively small boat, passengers are bound to mix and become more or less well acquainted, whether they be Lords and Ladies or just ordinary Middlewest Americans. It so happened that the English peerage was almost in predominance on our boat. Most of the men were Englishmen going to South Africa on business and a few — a very few of us — were Americans with "itchy feet" — if you know what I mean. The cultured English gentleman has a reserve that is very hard to penetrate but once you break through the crust he is the most friendly creature in the world. We were fortunate in being invited to a very swanky cocktail party in the ship's library early in the voyage, where we were the only Americans present. One man asked me where we were from. When the answer was "Kansas," he said, "It must be awfully wild out there!" He turned out to be "Sir Somebody," Baronet. Another time I was on the sundeck, taking pictures, and asked a man to pose for me for a foreground. I ordered him about a bit to get the right posture. This started a conversation in which I began telling him about the East Indies. "Yes," he said, "My grandfather was Governor-General of those islands." He turned out to be "Sir Somebody Else," and a well known name in the English peerage. So, you see, ignorance works both ways. Even among cousins.

II

Land of Promise

*I*T was a glorious restful trip down; but after fourteen days at sea we were glad to awaken one morning to find our ship anchored in the beautiful harbor of Capetown. You have heard the saying: "See Naples and die." That's all rot. I have seen half a dozen bays as beautiful as Naples and the one in which we lay that morning — with the white-walled, red-roofed buildings of Capetown terraced on a hillside above us, with the world-renowned Table Mountain in the background — made a picture one could never forget.

Capetown is, I think, the most underadvertised beauty spot anywhere. You think of it as just a great seaport town. As a matter of fact, it is not only the gateway for all South Africa, but it has more stability, culture and beauty than any of the other cities. It may not have the wealth or the size of Johannesburg, which is booming today more than any other city in the world; but if the United States should quit buying gold at fancy prices, "Joburg" now a city of a half million would soon look like Leadville, Colorado, on a Sunday afternoon. But that's another story, to come later.

Capetown is ideally situated on a high promontory, with the blue Atlantic on one side, and the even bluer (and certainly much warmer) Indian Ocean on the other. The Cape of Good Hope is only a few miles out of town and from its summit, about eight hundred feet above the sea, you can almost mark the line where the two oceans come together. As you stand on this elevation you cannot but think of the four hundred and fifty years of turbulent history of this romantic country, since those daring navigators, Dias and da Gama first sailed around the Cape seeking a new way to the riches of India and the far East. The drives around the Cape, following the shore line, are a revelation in beautiful scenery. The perfect roads winding along the mountain sides with frequent glimpses of the blue waters of the two oceans far below make one think of the French Riviera.

The city is extremely progressive. The University of Capetown, ideally situated on the hillside, a site selected by Rhodes, with acres of flower gardens and green lawns around it, commands a view of the whole city. It was founded by that great benefactor of all South Africa, Cecil Rhodes, and would do credit to any city in the world today. Every town and city in this part of the country seem to have gone in for fine hospitals, and Capetown has just finished an enormous one. Their nurses' home alone is as large as most of our American hospitals. I could go on and on with the beauties of this fair city until probably you would refuse to believe me; but I must say a word about the artistic or aesthetic side of the mixture of various races which comprise the city's population. The architecture is of many types; but the beautiful Cape Dutch Colonial predominates, especially in many of the finer residences. Occasionally an Englishman follows the traditions of the mother country and builds his home in good old English style with thatched roof and the inevitable flower garden; but the massive stone walls of the Dutch type with their cool white-washed sides seem more in keeping with the semi-tropical climate. In the downtown buildings and the many new apartment houses, everything is strictly modernistic. Parks, flower gardens, monumental arches and statuary are to be seen on every hand; but the colossal (not colossus) statue commemorating Cecil Rhodes, located high above the city, is perhaps the most noteworthy and impressive piece of bronze in South Africa.

This noble statue presents a horseman, typifying "Strength," reining in his steed. Every muscle is tense and he seems to be staring off into the future towards Rhodesia. Rising back of the horseman are a series of steps with pediments on either side, on which are crouched enormous British lions in bronze, like those around the Nelson monument in Trafalgar square. These steps lead up to a glorious Doric temple of white granite with a fringe of fir trees for a background. As Hedley Chilvers says in his *Seven Wonders of South Africa,* "It is a poem in stone (and bronze). It was here that Rhodes sat to dream. He looked down from around this spot on the broad rollers of the Indian and Atlantic oceans, breaking in ragged lines on opposite shores far below. One gets the brooding spirit of him here; in this high site; in this posthumous temple. He died at forty-nine after moving to wonderment half the world."

Down in the city I visited the modest little cottage by the sea where the great man spent his last days and where he uttered those last words which are sure to live forever: "So little done — so much to do."

Capetown is made up of a queer combination of races. There are the English, the Dutch, the Malays, East Indians, Jews, a few Americans, the Cape colored, and the Kaffirs (distinctly different) and many others. Do they mix? Do they co-operate? Do they love one another? They most emphatically do not! They cordially hate each other, always have and probably always will. At one period of his life Rudyard Kipling spent a good deal of time in Capetown and did some of his writing there. I think he must have been thinking of the population of Capetown when he wrote those lines: "East is east, and west is west, and never the twain shall meet."

Three or four days is not enough time to spend in Capetown, and although the delightful Mount Nelson Hotel tempts us to stay, we must be off for the interior, the gold fields and diamond mines, the great Victoria Falls, the wild animal country, and a thousand other sights; so we leave the Cape with many pleasant memories and the consoling thought that we will be back again after five weeks of eagerly anticipated adventure visiting the points of greatest interest throughout the Union.

We left Capetown one evening for the long journey to Bloemfontein, our first stop. It is two nights and two days by fast train — that is, fast for Africa. For the trains there are like the "mills of the gods;" they move slowly but they always arrive on time, probably because they have such slow schedules. Be that as it may, we were never more than ten minutes off schedule. Leaving Capetown the train winds slowly through the Hex River Valley, an exceedingly fertile fruit country, and up to the plateau of the great Karroo. The African Karroo resembles the pampas of southern Argentine or the desert of Arizona; it is a vast sandy plain with very little vegetation, and is as level as a floor as far as the eye can see. One might think that forty-eight hours of travel over a desert would be dull and monotonous, but with a comfortable compartment, good dining car service and plenty to read the time passed rapidly.

One thing I shall never forget happened on the second evening of our journey. It was on the Karroo that I saw the most gorgeous sunset I have ever witnessed. It seems that on the Karroo the wind blows the fine red sand of the desert into the air, where it is held suspended, and the light of the dying sun shining through it is refracted, and the red colors of an ordinary sunset are magnified to unbelievable brilliance until the whole vault of the heavens seems ablaze. Such a sunset, with the

29

blood-red colors on great banks of high-piled white clouds on the horizon, was ours that evening and as the light failed and the colors darkened, I thought of those charming lines:

> *Then winds her cloud-veils send her,*
> *And, where the light shines through,*
> *Red flames in skies of blue*
> *A purple glory lend her;*
> *And, robed in borrowed splendour,*
> *Night falls on the Karroo.*

It would never do for artists to paint tropical African sunsets; the critics would say that they had gone crazy with the heat.

After two days of the desert it was quite a relief to get into the high veld country and arrive at Bloemfontein, the chief city of the Orange Free State. There is nothing particularly interesting about this city, except that it is the Judicial Capital of the Union. It seemed queer to us that here in South Africa, they have a Judicial Capital, an Executive Capital and a Legislative Capital, each in a different city and widely separated.

Leaving Bloemfontein, the next hop was a short one, and we were off for Kimberley and the diamond mines. South Africa is without doubt the most prosperous country in the world today. The principal reason for this happy condition is that the country produces about sixty-five per cent of the world's gold (a very useful article these days) and ninety-five per cent of the diamonds. Now diamonds are not as popular as they used to be. Cheap costume jewelry has something to do with this; and then men are not bedizening their women folks as they used to do in more prosperous times. And so Kimberley is in a bad slump; and this little city whose name is a household word wherever diamonds are known is the one city in the whole country to decrease in population. This does not mean that the price of diamonds has fallen; as a matter of fact it is higher than ever but only because the whole output is virtually controlled by one big concern, the De Beers company. The reason for all this is that diamonds are becoming more and more plentiful. I was told that a few years ago new alluvial deposits were discovered, so rich that diamonds could be produced cheaper than glass. Whether this be true or not, the government co-operates with the De Beers Company in buying up and controlling these fields, thus saving the industry from price demoralization.

In Kimberley, we saw that immense abandoned hole in the ground — the great Kimberley mine. They don't mine that way any more. Diamonds are found in the blue clay of a great volcanic "pipe," which runs vertically into the ground — no one knows how far. Nowadays they run a narrow shaft down parallel with the "pipe," and tap it with transverse tunnels every so often. The best part of it is, that the further they go down the more plentiful the diamonds are. And so they mine them only as fast as the world will absorb them, while a few choice souls sit in London, or some other financial center, and determine the price every day. Sounds like a pretty fine business to be in, owning a diamond mine, but officials of the De Beers company in Kimberley told me it had not been profitable during recent years. You don't suppose they would be "spoofing" me, do you?

Now another long railway journey — to Bulawayo, in Southern Rhodesia, forty-one hours away by one of the South African railway's crack trains — made us realize how great the distances are in this vast country. While we are making this long railway journey, we have a good opportunity to discuss the South African railroads.

One of the great ambitions of Cecil Rhodes was to build a railroad from the Cape to Cairo, and the road was begun from Capetown with that end in view. But as they built northward, the gold fields called them one way, the diamond discoveries another and still other industries turned them aside and the road was never completed to Cairo, and perhaps never will be. Today a wonderful airplane service is making this trip twice a week, so a railroad may never be necessary. Practically all of South Africa's fourteen thousand miles of railroads are government owned and operated, and very successfully operated too. This is quite an admission from one who has always been opposed to government ownership of any common carrier and I might yet change my mind if I had to pay some of the high freight rates. But my experience journeying over these South African roads — eleven nights and I don't know how many days — over long stretches of desert, high mountains and deep valleys was a good test from a traveller's standpoint. The trains always left on time and arrived on time. The sleeping cars were very comfortable, and were like the European compartment cars, with a corridor down the side. There are no porters; you provide your own. These tireless servants, called "bed boys", are natives and they do everything for you. Even while we slept, our boy, Fred, whom we kept with us for five weeks, was pressing and cleaning our clothes, shining our shoes and doing a dozen other things to make us comfortable and presentable. Think of having a Pullman porter all to yourself! That's luxury; and they expect so little pay. But that is true of all native help. They do everything willingly and cheerfully, and are really fun to have about. It's one of the charms of Africa.

At a convenient station, as night approaches, the bedding in great canvas rolls is taken on the train and Fred proceeds to make up very comfortable beds. In the morning, it is rolled up again and dumped off at another station to be sterilized for another night's use. The drinking water provided in the sleepers is vile. It is highly tinctured with a yellow disinfectant, and so we bought mineral water from the dining car. The dining cars are very fair — not Fred Harvey's by any means, but much better than those of South American railroads and many of those in the Orient. Let me say again the South African railway travel is most comfortable, sometimes under very difficult circumstances. The officials are always kind and courteous and every one seems to do his utmost to make the traveller happy and comfortable.

32

Southern Rhodesia and Bulawayo at last!

I am fascinated with the name of that place; it sounds so African. And it is a typical central South African frontier town. The streets seemed ridiculously wide to us, about three hundred feet from curb to curb. When the early settlers laid out the town they made the streets this wide so that an eight span ox team could turn around without outspanning. Bulawayo is a thriving town and will undoubtedly, some day, be a good-sized city; but it is something more romantic that we have come here to see.

A few miles out of town rise the beautiful Matapos Hills, and it was the top of the highest peak, a spot that Cecil Rhodes called "World's View," that he chose for his own last resting place. And there his body lies today, in a tomb carved in the living rock, overlooking for miles, in every direction, the country he loved and served so well. Night and day, year in and year out, his old servants, at their own request, guard this place, the most sacred spot in all South Africa. Somehow, as one stands here, one involuntarily thinks of Stevenson alone on his mountain top in far away Samoa. The two men, so different in their walks of life, and yet so alike in the greatness of their souls. If Great Britain had done nothing but produce these two great men, that would be glory enough for her.

I could have lingered in the lovely Matapos Hills for days; but by this time the spell of Africa was going deeper into my veins, and one of the grandest sights of this wide world lay just ahead.

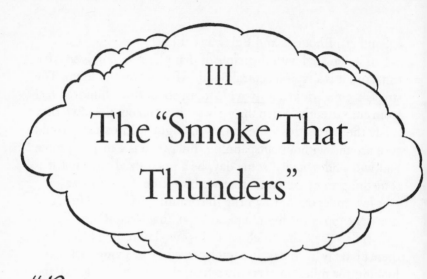

III

The "Smoke That Thunders"

"BREATHES there a man with soul so dead" who has not wanted some day to behold, with his own eyes, Victoria Falls? It was a night's ride from Bulawayo. The northern part of Southern Rhodesia is semi-tropical and when we awoke in the early morning, we looked out from the train windows on country entirely different from the high veld through which we had been passing for days. It was a jungle of tropical trees; a primeval forest; it really looked like the Africa of my dreams. Occasionally we caught glimpses of a native village or kraal; and when the train stopped at a wayside station, smiling black folk would offer us such souvenirs as wood carvings or the skins of wild animals.

Shortly after early breakfast, we arrived at Victoria Falls Hotel, one of the finest in all Africa; and as it was the "off" season we had the immense place almost to ourselves. From the front veranda we had our first view of the Falls; indeed, it was not far from this spot that David Livingstone stood in 1855 and beheld what no white man had ever seen before, this colossus of tumbling waters, Mosi-oa-tunya, or the Smoke-that-Thunders. The smoke, which can be seen for miles away is the mist or spray which rises in a white cloud from the tumbling waters to a great height above the falls. The thunder is, of course, the never ceasing roar of the cataracts. I will not attempt to describe Victoria Falls. Who can describe the indescribable? "In the presence of perfect majesty, perfect loveliness, language sinks into humble silence." Comparisons are odious, I know; but Victoria has almost twice the height of fall of Niagara, and about three times the width. There are no disfiguring signs, power-houses, or transmission lines at Victoria to mar its beauty. With the exception of the graceful railroad bridge which spans the river just below the falls, everything is just as nature made it.

The placid Zambezi river which marks the dividing line between Northern and Southern Rhodesia, flowing down from the jungles of the north, here makes a sheer drop of over four hundred feet; and after boiling through the rapids of the canyon for a few tortuous miles, proceeds on its leisurely course to the Indian Ocean. 1503974

Across the bridge is Northern Rhodesia and the little town of Livingstone. Just outside of Livingstone is a small wild animal reserve through which one may drive and see giraffes, zebras, antelopes and wildebeests; but we had come all the way to Africa to see big game in its natural habitat without a fence around it; so we were not interested. We were not far from the big game country; I had brought along my moving picture cameras with thousands of feet of film; and I was thirsting for blood. I wanted to get into the real wild game country. And lo! I found a way to gratify my ambitions by means of boat and plane.

HUNTING BIG GAME IN RHODESIA

Yesterday we went hunting on the upper waters of the Zambezi river, above Victoria Falls, for crocodile and hippopotami — and when I say hunting, I mean with cameras, *not* with guns!

We rode comfortably in a launch and the scenery was grand; but the game was scarce — owing to high water, they told us. I shot a couple of hundred feet of color film, got some wonderful tropical views, but only one "crock."

About the middle of the afternoon we landed on Candahar Island where, in the shade of the palms, the native boys prepared tea. Almost immediately we were surrounded by monkeys, swinging out of the trees and running up to make our acquaintance. On the island were wide tracks through the jungle, made by the "hippos" on their way to and from the river; but "Mr. Hippo" was not in evidence that day. Tropical birds and water fowl were everywhere, but I had come for bigger game.

So last night I engaged a plane to take us into the heart of the big game country, two hundred miles away, in Bechuanaland.

The pilot assured me that we would see many kinds of big game if we had any luck at all; and he promised to get me within "shooting distance" without having to use a telephoto lens. This sounded good to me; and we went to bed with instructions to be up before daybreak so that we could see the animals as they went to the water holes for their morning's eye-opener.

Did we sleep well? No. But principally because thunderstorms raged all night and rain fell in buckets.

But by five o'clock the storm had somewhat abated and the black "bed boy" came with our coffee and said, "Boss, de air man say 'come on!' He gonna try to make a start." And, though it looked very forbidding, my wife was game (for game) so I had to be.

In half an hour we were at the hangar, or rather at the place where it once stood, for it had been demolished the week before when a hundred-mile-an-hour hurricane struck here. Captain Spencer, formerly of the British Air Corps, our pilot, was awaiting us with a cheery good morning. "We had better go; the weather may not be so good tomorrow," he said. With some misgivings we climbed into his tiny De Haviland Moth plane; two black boys turned over the propeller; the Captain warmed her up a bit; and away we bumped over a very primitive landing field.

When we were well up we headed straight for Victoria Falls, to do what is called a "flip" over those roaring, tumbling waters. I will not attempt to describe my sensations for the next fifteen minutes. I have flown over the Grand Canyon of the Colorado for hundreds of miles, but that ride was tame compared to the "flip-flops" that little plane did over, under and around Victoria Falls. There was banking, circling, and side-slipping, and once we flew into the canyon close beside the falls at a forty-five degree angle, and all for my benefit — so that I could get good movies. Now that I have the pictures (and they are quite successful), I do not regret the year's growth I was frightened out of; but at the time how I did wish I were safely back in my little bed at the hotel!

At last we zoomed up, high above the spray, and headed straight north, following the course of the Zambezi River. We were now at an altitude of three thousand feet, and it was a marvelous thing to see the river dividing and uniting, again far below us. I had opened the window of the tiny compartment — the plane only held three people — and started grinding out pictures as soon as the plane had left the ground.

About fifty miles up the river we struck across the forest country, with nothing but trees below as far as the eye could see. "How about an emergency landing field?" came to my mind. "But 'there ain't no such animal in these parts' so forget it and enjoy the scenery. If the Lord had intended you to die in a plane crash, it would have happened two winters ago when you were lost in a storm for hours after nightfall, over the High Sierras." With this consoling thought, I lost my fears. After half an hour of flying over this thickly wooded country, the trees abruptly came to an end, and we could see a great plain stretching ahead.

I looked back, through a small window, to the pilot's seat. He sat there, intently peering first on one side, then on the other, never looking at his instruments. Finally he gave me a reassuring smile and started to dive; and in less time than it takes to tell we were skimming along the prairie, only about fifty feet above the

THE CATARACT, VICTORIA FALLS

ground. Then he banked and circled around a little stream so that I knew he had seen something that I was after. And, sure enough, on a sand bank in the middle of that stream were a dozen large "crocks" and two "hippos" sunning themselves. We circled three times while I pickled them in celluloid, and then we rose and straightened out again.

A few more miles and down we came again, this time to view the most amazing sight I have ever seen — a herd of hundreds of leechwe, animals of about the size and coloring of deer. We gave chase and had them running from us. I gave them both barrels as we passed over the herd, using slow-motion color film, sixty-four frames to the second, while my assistant was busy handing me unexposed cartridges. The Martin Johnsons had nothing on us!

On the next descent we found the plains literally alive with thousands of puku, an animal somewhat similar to the leechwe but larger and darker in color. Kudu, with their long spiral horns, were also to be seen. We were really in the big game country now. The territory beyond was sparsely wooded, and we saw a small herd of wildebeests frightened by the sound of the plane and charging in all directions like mad bulls. We could almost see the fire in their eyes. We didn't have the luck to see any of the spring-bok for which this country is famous; but we did see his next of kin, the reed-bok, which resembles our antelope.

Then we headed for the thinly timbered hills, where we saw a small herd of zebras, their black-striped tan bodies, visible for some distance. They ran helter-skelter up the hillside, while I got good shots of them without any mortality.

We had hoped to see elephants. But because the Duke of Northumberland, with whom we had travelled in the South Seas, had been shooting them the week before, they were now hiding out. But we had saved the best for the last. I remember some years ago, one of our circuses advertised giraffes. "Last three specimens in the world; when these are gone human eyes will behold them no more," we were told, so we went to the circus mainly to see these most curious animals. And here in Darkest Africa, only about seventy-five feet below us were dozens of those long-necked creatures, running from the sound of the plane's motor. So the statements on the circus poster were utterly discredited.

After this climax, we climbed to a great height again and started for home. The gasoline was getting low and there were no filling stations. We could see dark storm clouds ahead, too, and as we sped southward we were soon shut off from the earth by clouds. We were not above them, but in them, and of course without any radio or radio-beam. How that boy piloted that ship! It seemed a long and anxious journey home; and when the storm clouds lifted and we saw rising from the ground in the distance a white cloud which we knew was the spray high above Victoria Falls, we gave a long sigh of relief. We were almost home.

In another fifteen minutes Spencer was giving us another turn over the Falls, and we were heading into the landing field.

It was a great day, one we will never forget. Best of all, the pictures were quite successful and are visible proof of the truth of my story. Somehow, Africa has the power to make many dreams come true.

*   *   *   *   *

Surely Victoria Falls would be the high spot in anyone's trip to Africa. In one way it is like the Grand Canyon, for no matter how great your expectations are, it is even more grand and awe-inspiring than can possibly be imagined.

This was our furthest point north and we had now to double back through Bulawayo, and as far south as Mafeking, a name so familiar from Boer War days. At Mafeking our route was directly east, and we were soon in the Transvaal bound for Pretoria. We found Pretoria a delightfully quiet old Dutch city. It was the home of "Oom Paul" Kruger, and the house where he lived is now an interesting museum. Pretoria is the Administrative Capital of South Africa; and on a "kop," commanding a view of the whole city, the Union Buildings stand, probably the finest group in Africa. This is a city of flower gardens and flowering trees. I particularly remember the jacaranda tree, which we know in California. These trees, when in full bloom (and they seem to be blooming most of the time) are like huge blue bouquets; and the sight of them lining both sides of the avenue on the way up to the Union Building is unforgettable.

All South African cities are different from each other; each has its own individuality; just as San Francisco and New Orleans have in our country. Certainly stolid old Dutch Pretoria is like no other city. Just outside of Pretoria is Doornkloof, the country home of that Grand Old Man of South Africa, General Smuts.

It is an overnight train ride from Pretoria to the little village of Nelspruit, which was to be our jumping-off place for another adventure into the wilds of Africa. After breakfast at the quaint little Fig Tree Inn, where we were served by East Indian boys in white suits and turbans, we were ready for the long motor trip to Kruger National Park and more big game hunting.

Most people still think of South Africa as the "dark continent" of fifty years ago, a vast wilderness of jungle filled with an inexhaustible supply of big game. Nothing could be further from the truth. This country has made wonderful progress toward civilization in a short half century; and many of her cities and towns would put most of ours to shame in their civic improvements.

However, it is still the big game hunting paradise of the world; and its popularity as such, together with the accessibility of the hunting grounds by rail, motor car and airplane is rapidly depleting the wild life of jungle and plain.

With fine forethought the Africans are now doing what we have done in America — taking over vast areas as game reserves. One of them, Kruger National Park, where game of all varieties found in Africa is most abundant, comprises nine thousand square miles of mountain and plain.

41

The motor trip to the reserve is over winding roads and through hilly country. The country began to assume a wild aspect soon after we left Nelspruit. Little native kraals were perched on the hillsides; and occasionally we met some of the natives running along the roadside, armed with spears and leather shields. They had been out wild pig hunting, our guide informed us. They were clad only in breech clouts, with not even a smile on their sullen faces. They seemed to resent our invasion of their country and we felt like interlopers.

As we were crossing a wide plain under a blazing sun, an interesting thing happened. Away ahead of us I saw a car stalled in the road. "We had better stop and see if we can be of assistance," I suggested to our driver. Fortunately we were able to provide a much needed wrench; and while repairs were going on, an Englishman and his wife climbed out of the car and introductions followed. He proved to be that popular author, Francis Brett Young and, incidentally, his latest novel *They Seek a Country* was the best seller, almost everywhere at the time. To me, it seems the best historical novel yet written dealing with the strenuous pioneer days in South Africa.

We arrived at camp at about noon of a sweltering, tropical summer day in February. The rainy season was almost due but, fortunately for us, had not yet arrived. There are no hotels or lodges in Kruger's vast areas — only "rest camps" consisting of straw-thatched native huts or "rondavals," as they are called, and a large central hut where meals are served. The group of buildings is surrounded by a high wire fence and the gates are locked at dusk — no one is allowed in or out until the next morning.

Why is this? To keep out the lions! And the lions are never far away at any time.

We had rather a sketchy lunch at the camp mess and then a siesta until four o'clock (everyone rests during these hours, even the animals.) It is too hot during the middle of the day for man or beast to take chances with tropical heat and here, in the north-

"HE PUT HIS NECK OUT SO I SHOT HIM"

ern Transvaal, there is plenty of humidity, even at an elevation of thirty-five hundred feet.

At four o'clock our American-made car, with our guide-chauffeur, was ready, and we started with plenty of ammunition, cameras and film. (No guns are allowed in the reservation except for protective measures.) We were hardly through the gates when we saw animal life — a herd of wildebeests thrilled us. Later on we saw them in such numbers that we lost interest in them; they were as common as cows in Kansas. A jackal ran across the road just ahead; a beautiful steenbok and bushbok grazed a short distance away, but they are timid creatures and soon darted into the bush. Next we saw the roan antelope and sable antelope, both graceful animals. The buck or bull of the latter species resembles our elk and has similar antlers. A troop of wart hogs, ridiculous looking creatures, ran away before the photographer could get a close-up, then stopped and stared at us. The vividly striped zebras were seen in large numbers; they apparently like to be "taken." The air and ground were alive with tropical birds which looked as though they had escaped from a zoo — storks, flapwings, widow or weaver birds, greater bustards, toucans and secretary birds — to name only a few. Wild guinea fowl almost blocked the road.

Towards late afternoon, in the hills, monkeys and baboons ran about the rocks in great numbers, but there was no sign of the one animal we had travelled twelve thousand miles to see and, if possible, to photograph, namely the king of beasts, the lion.

The sun was setting — and what a gorgeous sunset, such as is seen only in South Africa! Suddenly there was a stir in the bush close beside us, the driver "froze the car," and we had a fleeting glimpse of a cheetah! But it was near dusk, and we had to be inside the compound before the gates closed or be out of luck, so we hurried on for camp.

Darkness comes quickly after sunset in the tropics; and after supper, whose *pièce de résistance* was springbok steak, the only

44

lights in the huts were oil lanterns so we sat outside, under the stars, and listened to the night sounds. First the tree frogs, cheery little fellows, tuned up. Then the jackals began their shrill, high call, much like the coyotes. Then a queer laughing sound we were told was the hyena; and finally, as Conan Doyle would say, "the long drawn cat call of the cheetah." It was a clear night, with heat lightning in the distance. The Southern Cross and a hundred million other stars were shining more brightly than I had ever seen them. This part of Africa has the clearest atmosphere in the world; and recognizing this fact our American universities have erected great observatories here.

The other noises had died down and we were about to retire when, suddenly, there was a terrifying roar not far away, and all our doubts as to there being lions in that vicinity were dissipated. We all know that the lion's roar is frightening enough, even though he be behind iron bars! These roarings kept up intermittently the whole night long, and certainly it was a comfort to know that we were safe inside the compound and not outside, wandering alone in the bush.

Getting-up time was just before dawn because we should be in the bush by daylight to see the animals on their way to the water holes to get their "morning's morning." A hurried cup of coffee and we were off. For three hours we saw many of our friends of the day before and made some new ones, but had no luck with Mr. Leo. Back to camp for breakfast. Then off again for a long drive to the Sabie river where, with luck, we might see hippopotami. And we did have luck; for just as we arrived at a glade at the river's edge, eight hippos, six enormous fellows and two babies, slid off the bank and began to bellow and snort and generally disport themselves, while a man from Kansas took fairly good closeups of the clumsy group. This was the only time while we were in Kruger that we were allowed out of the car away from camp, and then natives with guns were guarding us every minute.

Back to camp we went, again, for the heat was becoming unbearable and we had to rest for a couple of hours before leaving for the long drive through the mountains, back to civilization. It had been a wonderful experience but we had not seen what we had really come for.

At four o'clock we had left for a last look around and were not more than a quarter of a mile from camp when, from the driver's seat, I saw just ahead a lion — two lions — three — and then a fourth stalking along directly in front of us! I could hardly believe my eyes. We kept getting closer and closer until we were right upon them — four beautiful specimens.

As long as you are in a car, when lions are close, you are perfectly safe; but woe betide him who attempts to alight! It is a proceeding fraught with the utmost risk. Lions don't seem to mind the smell of gasoline; but they don't like the smell of man. I was grinding away on my pictures when more and more lions appeared, most of them immensely big fellows, and one mother with four cute little cubs. There were thirteen in all, the largest number seen at any one time for many weeks. Sometimes we were so close that one animal would fill the whole field of my finder. At other times I could get a group of several running along about twenty-five feet away. It was a busy time for me for about twenty minutes. As fast as I exhausted one magazine of my movie camera, my assistant was ready with a fresh one. My thoughts were running along three tracks: "What a lucky devil you are! Keep your camera steady or the pictures will show your nervousness! Will I ever get the films safely home?" It was almost too good to be true. Finally the lions seemed to have had enough of us, and they suddenly disappeared into the bush and the show was over. It was to be many weeks before the films could be processed and screened; but at last, back in America, they reached me safely. Imagine my joy when I found that they were well nigh perfect, and showed a fairly steady hand on the trigger during this thrilling experience.

RONDEVALS AT THE REST CAMP, KRUGER NATIONAL PARK

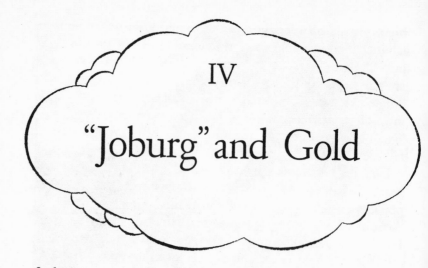

IV

"Joburg" and Gold

WE WERE BACK to civilization again. After partaking of a late dinner at the little Fig Tree Inn at Nelspruit, we entrained for the night's ride to Johannesburg.

There is a little word of four letters in the English language that either consciously or unconsciously plays an important part in the lives of all of us. No, it is not the word you are thinking of. It is Gold! In spite of the fact that most of the world has gone off the gold standard, this precious yellow metal is still the standard back of our own economic structure. The reason for this remark here is that Johannesburg is today producing on the Rand about sixty-five per cent of the world's supply of gold; and it seems the whole world wants the precious metal, with the United States usually the highest bidder. Naturally, this makes things very prosperous, not only in "Joburg," as they call it, but to a large extent all over South Africa.

One of the mine managers remarked to me, "We can't believe our good fortune. We don't understand it. Here we are, going down into a deep hole in the earth and bringing up the gold ore; smelting it and then selling it to your country at a ridiculously high price; then shipping it to the United States; only to have it buried there in another hole in Kentucky!" At the present high price the producers are not touching their high-grade ore, but are only working the low-grade veins, and regrinding the old dumps heretofore considered worthless. Of course they are working night and day to produce as much gold as possible, while the "getting" is good; so that, if and when the price drops, they can fall back to the high grade ore now being conserved.

Johannesburg has an interesting and exciting history. Fifty years ago it was only a few straggling shanties. Today it has a population of over half a million; is the largest city of South Africa, and is growing as fast as new buildings can be erected. It is a typical mining town on a grand scale. Everybody is excited and happy. Living is high, wages are high, and as yet they can see no end to their prosperity. Naturally, it is not altogether a beautiful city. The great white ore dumps, like miniature Alps, are to be seen just out of town in almost every direction; and, in the heart of the business district, a ramshackle building of the early days may be next door to a modernistic skyscraper.

Johannesburg can never be a beautiful city like Capetown; it has not the natural surroundings, but its citizens are making a valiant attempt to do everything that money can do to create beauty by civic improvement. They have some really good architecture in their public buildings, a fine university, one of the largest in South Africa, which confers all the major degrees, and strange to say a really good art gallery. The people of Johannesburg believe that, on account of its location the city is destined to be a great distributing point for a large territory long after its gold is exhausted.

We spent one morning at the Consolidated Reef Gold Mine, guests of the company, and were shown the interesting processes of stamping and refining the ore from the time it is hoisted from the depths of the mine until the pure golden button is taken from the crucible. Then we donned miner's clothes and were lowered

49

ON THE HIGH VELD IN THE TRANSVAAL

down a shaft eight thousand feet to the bottom of the mine. From this depth we followed along a tunnel for what seemed to be miles until we came to its head, where natives were drilling holes in the rock, using compressed air tools and preparing for a blast. The temperature would have been unbearably hot at this depth were it not for a supply of cold fresh air which must be pumped down constantly. It seemed as though we were down in the very center of the earth, and sunlight had never looked as good to us as it did when we were finally hoisted to the surface again.

These are the deepest mines in the world. They are down to about ten thousand feet in some of them now, and expect, eventually to reach a depth of twelve thousand feet. Think of working more than two miles below the earth's surface!

The city of Johannesburg lies directly over many of these mine workings, and there is a gradual sinking or slipping of the earth's surface above. And so every day one can feel an occasional jarring sensation, somewhat akin to an earthquake, as a section of the earth settles down to a slightly lower level. This was certainly a unique experience.

I think the fact that South Africa is a country of paradoxes is no better exemplified than in Johannesburg; at least it was there that the realization of it came to me most forcibly. In this country you may be one day visiting with the Bushman, most primitive of all living races; the next day you may be consorting with the best educated minds at the Witwatersrand University. In some parts of the country you may be forced to resort to the old ox team of pioneer days for your transportation; and at the end of your journey by this means you may find an express train or an airplane awaiting to take you the rest of your way. One night I was lulled to sleep by the roaring of lions in the jungle, the next I was in a great modern hotel, kept awake by the street noises of a busy city.

That's Africa! And that is the charm of Africa. One becomes tired of either extreme; and here it is so easy to step from one age to another, to exchange the sophistication of the city for the simple life of the country; it is so restful to step from the high-speed motor car to the slow dog-trot of the rickshaw of Durban.

After some days and nights of the life of Johannesburg, we were ready to explore more country far from the madding crowd.

The mountains were calling, and the beautiful Drakensbergs which range through Natal to the south of "Joburg" were only a night's ride away. We had been on the go for weeks, and we needed a few days rest and a change of scenery. So we heeded the words of John Muir, who said, "Climb the mountains and get good tidings. Nature's peace will flow into you as sunshine in trees. The winds will blow their own freshness on you, and the storms their energy, while cares will drop off like autumn leaves."

To reach the Natal National Park in the heart of the Drakensbergs, from the Transvaal, one must pass through historic Ladysmith, whose very name brings back memories of the Boer war. It was in this little town, where we spent the night, that the British soldiers, besieged for four long months, lost over three thousand men in that great adventure. But they were relieved at last; and that victory marked the beginning of the end of the war.

The next morning, as we drove out of town on our way to the Park, we passed by famous old Spion Kop, up whose sides so many British troops struggled and heroically died. The road over which we motored on the way to the Drakensbergs reminded me of one from Denver to our own Rocky Mountain National Park in Colorado. For miles and miles we drove beside fields of ripening corn, or "mealies," as they call it in Africa. In the meadows, hay was being cut and loaded on to wagons drawn by their sixteen patient oxen. Occasionally we would pass a small group of native huts with their round mud walls and wattled roofs baking in the sun, fat cattle standing in the shade of the thorn-bush tree, and always in the distance were the purple blue mountains, with white billowing clouds sailing above against the blue of the African sky. It was a photographer's paradise.

Leaving the smiling farmlands behind we began to climb through the foothills, and at last reached a high plateau surrounded by the jagged peaks of the Drakensberg range. And here, on a wooded knoll with a clear mountain stream rushing below, was the little National Park Hotel, where we were to spend several restful days and nights amid some of the grandest scenery in Africa. My literary ability is not sufficient to attempt a description of the grandeur of this region. In the mountains I invariably give up and resort to the easier way of letting the camera do the work. It is a land of towering mountain peaks and peaceful green valleys; land of splendid waterfalls and deep gorges, through which the infant Tugela River rushes on its long journey to the sea; land where one may ride horseback or climb mountain peaks to the heart's content; or sit restfully on the veranda of the hotel and watch the ever changing colors on the distant mountain tops. It is a land of brilliant sunshine, white drifting clouds, glowing sunsets and crisp nights; a place of welcome and rest after strenuous days of travel, where the black Basuto boys, who look after your creature comforts, are the most ideal servants in the world. No wonder it is the favorite playground of all South Africa.

Speaking of the black people of the Drakensbergs; they are descendants of the Bantu race and have come over the mountains from nearby Basutoland. They are readily distinguished from other tribes in that they invariably wear pink striped blankets. The native women of Africa carry everything on their heads, which practice gives them a very stately and erect carriage. They are apparently a cleanly people. One day I visited a native hut in which a large family was living. It was dark inside, windowless and odorless; and when my eyes became accustomed to the darkness I found it to be scrupulously clean. All of their cooking is done over outdoor fires. Sometimes on long walking or horseback trips I would hire a boy (usually a middle-aged man) to go along to carry my camera equipment. He would trot along beside

A SWAZI BOY

me all day, and in the end would be highly pleased indeed if I gave him a quarter.

Native labor is extremely cheap all over Africa; if this were not so, certainly Africa could not hope to maintain her present economic condition.

One day I met a native boy jogging along the road at a dog-trot. He had been running for miles and his perspiring body glistened in the hot sun. I stopped him to take his photograph and to converse. He was a Swazi warrior and carried the characteristic assegai and leather shield. "Where are you going?" I asked in very bad Swazi.

"To a wedding," he replied in good English.

I didn't ask him if he were the bridegroom; but from his belligerent accoutrements, I judged it might be an African "shot-gun" affair, and at least the wedding march should be "Onward Christian Soldiers, Marching as to War."

I always leave the mountains with a feeling of regret but we must motor back to Ladysmith and the amenities of civilization.

The all-day train trip from Ladysmith to Durban is undoubtedly the most spectacular one in all Africa. It runs through mountainous country, where, on account of the many steep grades, the road is electrified most of the way. At one point, where the road begins a descent of several thousand feet in a few miles, one may see from the car windows half a dozen loops of track winding down the mountain sides. In a great valley far below lies the lovely little city of Pietermaritzburg, founded by the Dutch in their Great Trek of the olden days. What a bloody history it has, and how vividly it is described in Young's *They Seek a Country!*

As the train approached Durban, we looked down on range after range of rolling hills as far as the eye could see. It is a land of mountain, forest and waterfall; it is the Valley of a Thousand Hills, with which we were to become better acquainted a few days later on a motor trip to Zululand.

The city of Durban, the capital of Natal, seems to me something like the city of Rio de Janiero in Brazil. It has the same languid charm of the sub-tropics as it lies basking in the dazzling sunlight along the blue waters of the Indian Ocean. Although it is a big city, it lacks the hustle and bustle of one; and, as you ride along the main thoroughfare in a rickshaw, its people seem to be taking life in a carefree, leisurely manner. Its queer population is made up of whites, natives and quite a large percentage of East Indians. We stayed at the delightful Marine Hotel, on the water front; and from the broad balcony of our rooms we had a grand view of the sparkling waters of the bay, upon which ride every manner of craft, from the tiny row-boat to the great ocean liner. In the hotel I was served, not by the native black boys, who addressed me as "Baas," to which I had become accustomed; but by East Indians in white linens and turbans, and I was now "Marster." The East Indians lacked the winning smile of the black boy but they were just as polite and efficient. What a joy it was to give the merest signal, and to have a silent servant appear to gratify most respectfully my every want. I felt as though I were living in the atmosphere of the Arabian Nights.

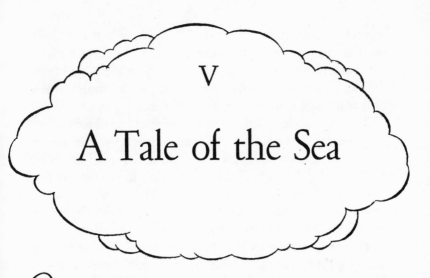

V

A Tale of the Sea

ONE CAN hardly sail the Seven Seas, as I have been doing for the last ten years, in the safety and comfort of a modern steamship, without standing in awe of those pioneer navigators who sailed into the unknown in tiny crafts not larger than the lifeboats of present times. Today, with every sea carefully charted; with the radio keeping ships in touch with the world every minute; and with electrical devices — autogiros and the like — which virtually run the ship by themselves, ocean travel has become perhaps our safest means of transportation. One is far safer on the stormy deep than in crossing the street in his own home town.

In Norway, a few years ago, I saw the remains of a Viking ship which had recently been dug out of the deep sand of the beach upon which it had been wrecked many centuries before. It was not much more than a glorified canoe; yet it was in just such a frail craft that old Leif Ericson, long, long before the days of Columbus, sailing from island to island, without benefit of compass, and with only the stars to guide him, crossed the stormy north Atlantic and discovered America, or at least touched its northern shore. But the Norseman was never a good propagandist; and so, long afterward, when Columbus, with the proceeds from the sale of Isabella's jewels, followed the comparatively quiet southern waters and discovered islands in the West Indies, he sailed home with positive proof that he had found a new world and all of Europe soon knew about it.

But to come back to today and the palatial ferry boats which patrol the far corners of the maritime world — the age of romance, of risk and daring on the sea, seems over; but is it?

One morning I awoke in my room facing the bay at the Marine Hotel in Durban, on the east coast of Africa, and saw, in the blue waters of the Indian Ocean, which here form a safe harbor, a small ketch, or two-masted sail boat.

Nothing unusual about that! The bay was full of boats of every description, but from the stern of this tiny craft floated a diminutive American flag!

No matter how much you have travelled in foreign countries, nor how blasé you may have become after months of absence from home on the other side of the world, the sight of that little piece of bunting never fails to send a thrill up and down the old spine, as only those who have experienced it can understand.

What, I wondered, can that little boat be doing here — seven thousand miles from home by the nearest sailing route?

Keen with curiosity, I took my cameras and hired a native boy at the dock to row me out to investigate. I arrived alongside to find the deck deserted.

"Ship ahoy!" I called, in landlubbery fashion and, almost immediately, two bronzed heads appeared above the hatchway.

"I'm from Kansas, U. S. A.," I said.

"We're from Iowa. Come aboard for breakfast," they replied.

Climbing on deck, I was greeted by two handsome, athletic boys, wearing only Javanese batik sarongs, their bodies tanned to a copper shade by many tropical suns. Down in the roomy cabin of this thirty-foot boat, a black boy ("the cook and the bosun too") made the third of this gallant crew. He was soon serving hot coffee — good coffee — while we sat on wide bunks around the big center table, lit our cigarettes and began what turned out to be three hours of most interesting conversation. The talk started on the common ground of photography, the skipper being an expert amateur, and then by degrees and digres-sions they told me their story.

They were Des Moines boys and, by coincidence, I knew the father of one of them, the president of a bank in that city. After being graduated from Drake University, they had decided to seek adventure and to see the world in a most unusual way before settling down to the humdrum life of business careers. And so they went down on the lower Mississippi and built the "Hurri-cane" with their own hands. Kauffman, the older of the two and the skipper, had had some experience in sailing in Florida waters. Meffert, the mate, had never seen the Ocean! One fine day, with a Mexican boy as a cook, they sailed out of the river and into the Gulf to see the wide world, with all the confidence and courage of those Norse Vikings of old.

That was in April, 1935. Now, after three years of travel, they had put in at Durban, Natal, because the cook was taken ill with malaria.

"Where have you been, boys?" was one of my first questions.

" 'Where haven't we been?' would be much easier to tell," they replied in unison.

"First we sailed across the Caribbean Sea, and then we were piloted through the Panama Canal. The pilot who took us across the canal said that he would rather take through a battleship, than a seventeen-ton ketch such as ours."

Arriving upon the Pacific side they made for the Galapagos Islands, where they cruised around, taking pictures for two and a half months. Then to Tahiti, Samoa, Fiji, the New Hebrides, New Zealand, Australia and then north and west to the East Indies. After touching at Lord Howe Island they were ship-wrecked on a coral reef forty miles from Samarai.

59

"The currents are uncharted there and we ran aground at night," the skipper explained. "Planks were ripped out of the vessel and it seemed that we would have to abandon the voyage. That forty miles to Samarai was completed in the yacht's small dinghy (a row boat to us Kansans.) It could only have been accomplished in fine weather."

Two boats and some natives were chartered at Samarai and the little ship was salvaged after six days on the reef. The voyage continued through the Dutch East Indies to Singapore, where a complete refit was necessary. From Colombo the long journey of nearly four thousand miles to Zanzibar was made safely.

Their happiest time was spent in the South Sea Islands, at a little island called Bora Bora where they stayed as guests of the native chief for some weeks. The mate showed me a picture they had taken of the chief's beautiful daughter. Maybe this had something to do with the length of their stay! Men and women often swam out to their boat with presents and the visitors enjoyed unlimited hospitality. Such are the romantic South Sea Islands that are still off the beaten track.

"Haven't you experienced some bad storms in these typhoon waters?" I enquired.

"We certainly have," replied the skipper. "Then we trim her down to the minimum of sail, just enough for steering, and ride her out. We have lost some masts and spars in those storms; but don't forget that we have kept almost constantly south of the equator and in the southern seas, unless you get too far south, the weather is good ninety per cent of the time."

"And where next from here?" I asked.

"Home for Christmas!" they chorused. "Of course we will have to take it slowly in order not to strike the West Indies at hurricane time, but even then we should be back by late fall."

Back of the wide bunks were two long shelves of books; on the center table maps and charts were scattered about; up through the hatchway I caught a glimpse of the new native boy cook moving about on deck. Somehow there was the flavor of Joseph Conrad about the whole thing; and the story of *The Nigger of the Narcissus* flashed through my mind.

It was nearing lunch time and I rose to go.

"Better come with us and take over the photography," they said. "We are writing articles for a Chicago paper and they have to be illustrated."

What a compliment!

"No, boys, I am too old and too cowardly to accept, and I am too used to riding in a sea-going hotel," I told them.

"You won't forget to write our dads, will you? They won't believe it when we write that we are O.K., but perhaps they may believe you."

Out on deck I photographed them in color movies and then stepped into my boat to go ashore. As we rowed away I called back: "You look like football men to me."

"Sure," they yelled back, "Drake University. You are always beating us."

"Not always. You're beating this troubled old world right now at any rate!" I answered as we waved final good-byes.

And so I left them, modern Vikings who had set forth to see the world without benefit of radio or steam, and with only small knowledge of navigation. But they are having experiences that do not come to one in a million; and, although they may be rich men's sons, they are paying their way with their writing.

In Lincoln Ellsworth's book, *Beyond Horizons,* he writes: "He who has trodden stars seeks peace no more." Certainly these two boys have trodden stars for almost three years; and if they get home safely, life in Des Moines is going to be pretty dull and uninteresting for some time afterward. But surely, men who have the courage to do what they have done will somehow, some way, go on doing interesting things for the rest of their lives. At any rate, they have demonstrated that the spirit of the Vikings still lives, even in America today.

61

A ZULU DANCE

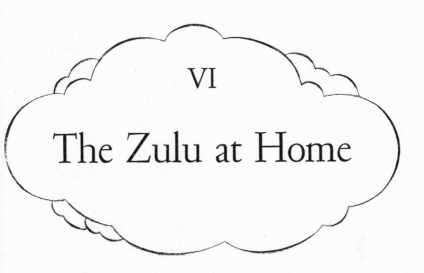

VI

The Zulu at Home

A GOOD MANY years ago, a young American missionary doctor came to Durban to start his life's work of healing the sick Zulus. His first hospital was a room in a little three-room cottage in which he lived. The Zulus, as they became Christianized and gave up their witch doctors, began to come to him in such numbers that the house overflowed with patients and he had to put them on cots out in the yard. From this humble beginning the work grew and grew, until, today, the McCord Zulu Hospital is one of the largest and finest in Natal, and is probably the only hospital entirely devoted to the treatment of the Zulus anywhere. A mutual friend had given us a letter of introduction to Dr. McCord; and when I telephoned him he came in his car to take us to see the crowning glory of his life's work. The hospital, a fine piece of modern architecture, ten stories high, stands on a hill overlooking the city, and is a model of what a modern hospital should be. Dr. McCord and his good wife, who has been a real helpmate in building this great institution, spent hours in showing us every department he and his large staff are conducting. The good doctor is getting along in years and most of the work is left to younger men now, but as we went from ward to ward, he seemed to know all of the patients and as he passed by, the expression in their eyes was as though they were looking at a god. I am proud to know this quiet, modest, saintly man, who has devoted his whole life to the relief of the sufferings of a noble race. Truly Dr. McCord is the Father Damien, the Sir Wilfred Grenfell, of South Africa.

When I was a boy, the word Zulu struck terror to my heart. I visualized the naked Zulu warriors dancing around a large kettle over a fire, in which was cooking a nice fat missionary. The Zulus to be seen in Durban today are a most fascinating lot of people — not at all belligerent. The rickshaw boys are dressed up, probably to attract customers, in gaudy and elaborate costumes of every color of the rainbow. Their bodies are clothed mostly in bracelets and bands of beads, but their principal adornment is a towering headdress of feathers, of every hue, out of which invariably protrudes an immense pair of horns, which gives them a look of something between man and beast. The women in the native market, especially those who have come in from the country, are most picturesque. The universal costume, aside from beads and bangles, which they wear in great profusion, is a short black skirt, reaching from below the waist half way down to the knees. Around the breasts, which are astoundingly well developed, is always worn a narrow band of beads, for just what purpose I was never able to discover. Their headdresses are sometimes a foot high and marvelous to behold. They are dome-like structures of black wool or hair, held in place by skewers of porcupine quills thrust in from all directions.

But to see the Zulus properly, one must go to Zululand, where there are 250,000 of them scattered over a vast territory, living in their primitive state. And for this purpose we went to Zululand.

This country lies in the hills almost directly north of Durban and it is about a three hour motor drive to its southern border. The road leads up into the Valley of a Thousand Hills; and

RICKSHAW BOY, DURBAN, NATAL

when we reached its summit we had a stupendous view of the country in all directions — undulating hills, one after another, literally by the thousand, all clothed in a lovely purple haze. And far, far away a faint gimpse of the Indian Ocean. At last we turned off the main travelled road and started bumping over a very poor one. We were in Zululand. After some miles of such travel, we arrived at a sort of trading post which was to be the gathering place that day for a big Zulu dance, with the natives coming from all over the neighboring country. We had arrived early so that I had time to set up my cameras at an advantageous spot. Soon we saw and heard the natives coming from all directions. The warriors and the maidens marched in single and double file, chanting their tribal music as they kept step. It reminded me of the dances of the American Indians in New Mexico.

They gathered in long lines and made ready for the dance. I have witnessed native dances in many parts of the world, in far off Bali and in Fiji, in Samoa and in Java, in wild New Guinea and Siam. I have been watching the tribal dances of our North American Indians for years, but I don't believe I have ever seen any dancing to compare with that of the Zulus. Their costumes consisted of not much of anything and a little bit of everything, if I may be paradoxical. The little bit of everything was beads, bracelets and anklets in great profusion; a circlet of lion or monkey fur here and there; feathers of many varieties; and a little cloth around the loins. Everything they wore was of the brightest color imaginable, and no color was missing. The music or sound was furnished by the rhythmic beating of ox-hide covered drums, the blowing of shrill whistles, and the clapping of hands; and added to all this was the chanting of tribal songs.

The dancing was symbolic but there was nothing lewd or suggestive about it. There was a great deal of posing and gesticulating and extremely quick kicking of the legs, the shiny black bodies always swaying in perfect unison with the rhythm of the music. They would start with a slow tempo which gradually

66

A ZULU BELLE

became faster and faster until they would fall to the ground in almost a frenzy of exhaustion. It was hotter than blue blazes and, as the dancers warmed to their work, their bodies glistened with perspiration and the mutton tallow they had applied beforehand. They would dance in chorus and then some man or woman would step out in front and do a solo dance, each one distinctly different from the others. They kept this up for hours until finally they formed in lines again, and went jogging off over the hills in the various directions from whence they had come, and the show was over.

The Zulu is a dignified person and haughty of demeanor. He is an acknowledged aristocrat among all the Bantu people. There is none of that happy-go-lucky attitude of the American negro about him; but, like the Indian, he believes that women were made for work and men were made for war — and now that there are no more wars — well, he is simply the general manager. They are magnificent physical specimens. The men are sparely built and muscular and the women develop a very stately carriage from carrying everything on the head. They are a polygamous people. The number of wives a man possesses is significant of his wealth and social position. A man buys a wife for a certain number of cattle; the comelier the woman the more cattle he has to pay for her. I met and photographed a Zulu who had seven wives. He rode in state in his ox cart, while the women trudged along behind carrying the burdens.

One day as I stood out on Lighthouse Point, in the harbor of Durban, watching the ships sail out, bound for ports far away, I saw a tiny speck in the northern sky. As I watched, it grew larger and larger until I could hear the hum of motors. Finally it came roaring overhead, made a huge circle, and then, like a great white swan, dropped smoothly to the quiet waters of the bay.

It was the mail plane from England, only five days out of Southampton! Shades of Cecil Rhodes and his dream of a railroad from the Cape to Cairo!

68

IN THE DRAKENSBERG

Here today are flying boats which carry mail and passengers from London to Capetown regularly twice a week in six and a half days; and they are planning now to cut this time to four and a half days.

As a matter of fact, practically all first class mail leaving South Africa today goes by air. To send an air mail letter to England costs a penny and a half, or three cents in our money. To send one to any place in Canada, twelve cents our money; but to send an air mail letter to New York costs a shilling, or about twenty-five cents, and of course from England across the Atlantic it must go by boat. To any point west of New York the rate is a shilling and a half, or thirty-seven cents! Sounds like a "gyp," doesn't it? The Americans living down there certainly feel that way about it. Added to this, they claim that letters to America are delayed in England for days, so that the British merchant has a great advantage in time saved in delivering his goods to his African customers. Be that as it may, Yankee ingenuity has found a way to beat it in the following manner. The Yankee sends his letter to his agent in England at the three cent rate. The agent simply tears off the outside envelope, puts on a five cent stamp, and remails it to the States and the letter goes all the way for eight cents instead of a quarter, without any undue delay in England.

The time had come for departing from Durban, and the motor vessel "Athlone Castle," the pride of the Union Castle Line, was waiting to take us south to East London, our next port of call. As we sail down the east coast of Africa over the calm waters of the Indian Ocean, it is a good time to answer some of the questions that have been asked me about the South African natives.

As has already been stated there are about ten million people living in South Africa today and of this population less than two million are white, while there are about eight million natives. In other words, the blacks outnumber the whites four to one. The black man is not a slave, but his is a subjected race. He is unquestionably badly treated and poorly paid. The white man

70

RED BLANKET BANTU GIRL NATAL

claims that, if it were not for cheap labor, South Africa could not exist from an economic standpoint. The black man is a simple soul. He works hard when it is necessary, and takes what he can get. He has not learned about labor unions, sit down strikes, or walk-outs as yet. He is not a menace from a fighting standpoint as in the olden days, but he is a social and economic problem. He is increasing in numbers far faster than his white neighbor, and is, in many instances, drinking in education. He is no longer the little brother, but is fast becoming a man. What is his future? That is the big question which worries all South Africa.

Since coming back from South Africa, a great many people have asked me: "What kind of language do they speak there?" South Africa is bi-lingual. The English, of course, speak their own language while the Dutch, or rather the Boers, speak Dutch. In addition there is a new language called "Africaans," a kind of kitchen Dutch adapted to African use which has many words not in the Dutch language. Africaans has been adopted as an official language and is now taught in the schools. It is becoming more and more used, and it is the hope that eventually it will become the universal language of the country. A great many of the natives are now tri-lingual. They speak their own tribal language, they have a working knowledge of Africaans and they also speak English if they come much in contact with English speaking people. In my limited contact with the natives, I formed the impression that they are natural born linguists.

One more subject which I should like to treat is that of education. South Africa is certainly an up and coming country in the matter of schools — schools, that is, for the white races. They have fine universities, agricultural colleges, technical schools, high schools and grade schools, but, as a rule, they are not for the black people. This is not to say that there are not many schools for the natives. There are, but the general feeling seems to be that if you educate a black man, you spoil him for the purpose for which he was intended — namely, to be a common laborer.

The black man has no vote and no representation from his own race in parliament; he is not a slave; but on the other hand, he is in a state of semi-serfdom, which, in some industrial locations, is not far from being slavery.

The day after sailing from Durban, we arrived at the dear little town of East London. The principal thing I remember about our visit there was an exhilarating drive into the farming country. One must keep in mind that along the eastern coast the land is very rich and fertile and the vegetation is almost tropical. Here we saw an entirely different native people, called the Red Blanket tribe. These people white-wash their faces, which gives them a very grotesque appearance.

From East London, the boat took us to Port Elizabeth, a thriving English town which, in time, is bound to be one of the principal seaports of the eastern coast. From this place we were scheduled to visit the Addo Bush Elephant Reserve; but because the elephants were on the rampage and had killed one of the game wardens a few days before, we were forbidden to enter, so consequently my acquaintance with the elephant is still confined to the circus and the zoo. We did visit a snake farm, but I have seen better ones in Siam and Brazil, so the sight here did not thrill me. It was exciting, however, the next day, while driving along a country road, to see an immense cobra, one of the deadliest of all snakes, glide across the road just ahead of us.

We abandoned our ship at Port Elizabeth and took to the train again. Another overnight trip to little Oudtshoorn, a Dutch town in the heart of the Little Karroo. Here again the country is naturally barren but as in our own western lands — where irrigation makes everything possible — so here, the country round about "blossoms like a rose." Away back in the "gay nineties," Oudtshoorn enjoyed a splendid boom. It was the center for ostrich farming. But because the "swift" speed of the early open automobile made it impossible for the ladies to wear waving feathers in the wind, ostrich feathers "went out," presumably

73

forever, unless some new use is found for them, such as more Sally Rands! However, ostrich farms still exist, a number of them close to town. We went out to visit one of the largest in the whole country, where we saw these great birds by the hundreds, from the little ostrich chicks just hatched, up to the fullgrown ostriches in great herds.

I asked the owner of the farm why he continued to raise ostriches if they were unprofitable.

"For the same reason that you raise fine dogs or horses in your country. For the satisfaction of breeding better animals!" was his answer.

He had plenty of other products that were profitable, he said, among them twenty tons of fine honey which was to be bottled next day. It was a grand old plantation, much like those of the old South, and under the shade of a huge pepper tree we had tea and scones, served by white capped and aproned black servants. While I hunted for pictures, the host loaded the other members of the party with fine ostrich plumes; presents which in the old days would have been princely gifts. Out on the front lawn the bees were humming over the flower beds; through the trees I could see the great, long-necked ostriches strutting in the fields; and in the far distance, the glorious Swartzberg range shimmered in the noonday sun.

That afternoon we made a visit to the great Cango Caves, which to put it succinctly, left us cold. We had been spoiled by the grandeur of the Carlsbad and other great caves back home.

If you ever go to South Africa, be sure that you take the route we have been following since leaving Capetown; it works up gradually to a crescendo; while if you should go in the opposite direction it would indeed be an anti-climax. Our next two days were spent in auto travel over the superb Garden Route, and — most certainly as far as beautiful scenery was concerned — we had saved the best for the last. I say last, for we were now headed for Capetown and, alas, the end of the inland trip.

74

Leaving Oudtshoorn, we entered the parched Karroo once more, and for miles and miles we might have been in Arizona; except that instead of cactus, we had the tall white flowering aloe, which resembles the tree-cactus. Its green and white shades were very effective against the desert purples and the hazy blue of the distant mountains. Before long we were in the hills, and the road wound up and through gorge and forest. Our objective was the lovely district of the Knysna and the sea again, but to get there we must climb several thousand feet over Prince Alfred Pass, and then descend a winding precipitous road through a heavily wooded mountain district.

One should have some knowledge of the trees and flowers of his country before travelling through it. It is a flower-lover's paradise. A list of the wild flowers one sees by the road would sound like a page from a book on botany. I shall not attempt to enumerate them, but I must mention the gigantic yellowwood trees and the stinkwood trees from which the early Dutch made their ponderous furniture. Along the roadside were great banks of many varieties of ferns, and clumps of the pink and brown protea, South Africa's national flower. White, pink, red and purple heather, such as was never dreamed of in Scotland, grew to the height of small trees. It seemed like a mist of soft color blowing in the wind.

At last we descended a mountainside, and saw the cobalt blue of the sea far below us, with the great rocks of the Knysna Heads jutting out from the shore line. The next day's ride was almost a repetition of the day before, except that the country and the views were still more lovely. The everturning and winding road led through fine farm lands, up over steep mountain passes, and down again into fertile valleys. Every mile or so along the dusty road we passed long ox teams — sixteen patient animals drawing a great lumbering cart, always with a boy at the head to guide them, and a man at the rear with a long pole with which to goad them. Here we see typified the very spirit of South Africa.

75

Towards nightfall we came to the Wilderness, and again to the ocean, and here we rested for two days at one of the finest seaside resort hotels in all Africa. It seemed a heavenly place to rest and relax after days of strenuous travel. The weather was ideal; and there was a broad sandy beach close by, with great breakers rolling in from the Indian Ocean which seemed to call us to come and bathe. One morning a young man, who had been my travelling companion and fellow photographer for weeks, and I decided to go for a swim. I am not a strong swimmer and I soon discovered that there was a dangerous undercurrent so I came out and settled myself upon the beach. And then the tragedy occurred!

A cry for help came from my friend, far out in the water!

Two strong swimmers, who were in the water near him at the time, did everything that was humanly possible to rescue the drowning man but all in vain. It was days before the sea gave him back. This unfortunate catastrophe was the only incident which marred the pleasure of the entire trip.

That night we drove to George, a serene little English town which Anthony Trollope declared to be "the prettiest village on the face of the earth." And from George we took the train back to Capetown.

We had left Capetown in the late evening; we came back on a bright fall morning. It was our last look at inland South Africa, and it left a vivid impression on my mind. We sped through a rich farming country, with ripening crops on every hand; sleek cattle were in the pastures; and the farmers were busy gathering the fall crops. The well-kept farm houses and barns were surrounded by tall and graceful eucalyptus trees; and in the distance cloud-capped Table Mountain told us we were near our journey's end.

VII

Farewell to Africa

*A*T THE Capetown wharf, the "Athlone Castle," in which we had travelled part of the way down the eastern coast, was waiting for us; and all too soon we were on board and prepared to say farewell, regretfully indeed, to bewitching, sun-blessed South Africa, where everyone had shown us such unfailing kindness and friendship.

As we sailed out of the harbor and looked for the last time on historic Table Mountain, looming in the background, with a table-cloth of white clouds spread over the level surface of her top, I consoled myself with the thought so truly expressed in that old Arab proverb, "He that hath drunk of Africa's fountains will drink again."

"South Africa is a rich land," to quote Dorothea Fairbridge in the *Pilgrim's Way*, "dowered by the sun with all the fruits of the earth, carrying in her bosom treasures of gold and diamonds, bearing in her arms yellow sheaves of corn and grapes for the wine pressing. A land made for health, wealth and happiness, needing only peace and unity to make her the most radiant jewel in the Empire's crown of jewels."

But will she ever find that peace and unity? For many years to come South Africa is bound to be a country of racial problems. Imagine, if you can, our country peopled by four times as many colored as whites; colored people whose problems were entirely different from our own. Then imagine a President representing one party and a Congress looking after the interests of another party, and you would have exactly the situation in South Africa today. Eventually, the political differences between Briton and Boer may die out; but the problem of doing the right thing by the black man is a much more serious and lasting one. Unquestionably, the white man has been a tyrant; and there are plenty of "Simon Legrees" in Africa today. One cannot travel far without observing instances of such domineering.

Anthony Trollope went to South Africa back in 1877 and studied the country thoroughly. When he returned home, he wrote a book, concluding with this statement: "Africa is a country of black men — and not of white men. It has been so, it is so, and it will be so." Whether he was right or whether he was wrong, no one can tell. South Africa's sociological fate is in the lap of the gods; and no one is wise enough, in these days of universal greed and hatred to foretell Destiny. The reader will forgive these cogitations here. They are from notes made on the long ocean voyage back to England when impressions, gathered on the trip, were fresh in my mind.

This old world of ours is changing rapidly. During the past quarter century more changes have taken place than in ten times that period previously. Of course, it is all due to modern fast communication and transportation and I, for one, don't like it. Everything and every place is becoming modernized, commercialized and, worst of all standardized, at a rapid rate. The interesting, the picturesque, the unusual is giving way to the commonplace. Someday, I suppose, the people all over the world will be wearing the same kind of clothes, as far as the climate permits, living in the same kind of houses, and speaking the same language.

During the last ten years, I have seen blocks of modern apartment buildings in Budapest, in Berlin, and in London, and they were exactly the same as those I saw in Sidney, in Buenos Aires and in Shanghai. Have all the architects of the globe been regimented? At least there seems to be no chance for them to express any individuality or originality in their work. How uninteresting the world is going to become in a few more decades when every man's house is exactly like his neighbor's house; when the people of Japan live like the people of India; or when the Kaffirs of Africa eat, talk and dress as do their black-skinned brothers in far-off New Guinea.

And so I give thanks that I have seen China at a time when the men still wore skirts and the women pantaloons. I am glad that I visited the beautiful island of Bali before it was spoiled by cruise parties; and finally I thank God that I have seen at least a part of that mysterious, romantic, individualistic South Africa before some Hitler or Stalin comes along and spoils it forever.

Of the friendships made in South Africa I must mention very briefly only a few. First a young Englishman, now living in Capetown, a Mr. Cowlard (what a name! I always called him Bullbutter!) who was my guide, philosopher and friend during the whole inland journey. You couldn't find a better companion.

One day I wandered into a bank in Port Elizabeth, to get some information. It was about ten o'clock on a Saturday morning, the busiest time of the week for a banker. The president, a native of South Africa, born of British parents, asked me to come back to his private office, where we soon discovered that we had many things in common. We talked of "ships and shoes and sealing wax," of mortgages and things, until I suddenly realized that it was almost one o'clock! I was apologizing, when he asked:

"Well, what are you doing tomorrow?"

"Nothing in particular," I replied.

"I will be around for you with my car at ten o'clock to show you the country, if you like."

He was as good as his word. We drove all over the country and I gathered a world of valuable first-hand information from him. We parted at eight o'clock that evening and I shall never forget his friendship and hospitality.

One more instance of good will. It happened the day of the terrible tragedy of the drowning of my friend at the Wilderness. I was endeavoring to make arrangements for the care of the body, should it be recovered after we left. A very distinguished looking elderly Englishman stepped up to me and asked if he might be of some assistance.

"Pardon my intrusion at such a time," he said, "but I happen to be in some authority here in South Africa and can possibly be of some help."

He explained that he was one of the four English directors of Cook's. He was General Sealyham during the Boer war, is now Lord Mottestone, of Mottestone Castle, Isle of Wight, and King's Counsellor. This introduction led to a long conversation, after which we went to meet Lady Mottestone. In the end, he was able to be of great assistance in making various arrangements, and in parting he said, "If you ever come to the Isle of Wight, be sure to make us a visit at Mottestone Castle."

I had been told, before going to South Africa that the people there hated Americans. Quite on the contrary, I never visited a country where everyone was so cordial, so friendly and hospitable. In fact we did not have one disagreeable experience with the white or the black people on the whole trip.

We met any number of the British peerage on the boats coming and going, and invariably found that those whose titles were newly acquired were inclined to be snobbish, and those who were "to the manor born" were just the opposite.

The long six thousand mile trip back to England was over a quiet, restful sea all the way, but after fourteen days' sailing it was good to find we were back in the English Channel and would be in London that afternoon. It seemed like home again.

VIII

Springtime in England

"Oh, to be in England now that April's there."

THESE LINES OF Browning's were ringing in my heart when I awoke one April morning in London, after returning from a twenty-thousand mile journey by sea and by land into the heart of Darkest Africa. I had been in London three months before, in the dead of winter, and it had been cold, raw and uncomfortable, and I had had a very unhappy time. True, the winds had been sharp only the day before, when I took a launch up the Thames, to watch eight brawny young oarsmen from Cambridge row against eight brawnier young oarsmen from Oxford in their annual boat race. But that was yesterday, and today was the kind of day that poets rave about; the kind that must have inspired Browning when he wrote those lines:

> *"The year's at the spring*
> *And day's at the morn;*
> *Morning's at seven;*
> *The hillside's dew-pearled;*
>
> *The lark's on the wing;*
> *The snail's on the thorn:*
> *God's in His heaven —*
> *All's right with the world!"*

Why didn't the good man write more of this kind of poetry, which clings in one's memory forever, rather than those obscure verses which no one really understands. I am sure that the "Pied Piper" will be piping and "Pippa" will be passing long after "Paracelsus" is forgotten.

I know my England fairly well and I am on rather intimate terms with old Chaucer; but, strange to say, I had never made the pilgrimage to Canterbury! And if there is anything in the world I dote on, it is the English Cathedrals. I think that, collectively, they are the loveliest examples of fine architecture in the wide world.

And so I decided that this was just the kind of day to make a pilgrimage to the famous old cathedral city. First, breakfast of tea and toast and marmalade and — it being Sunday morning — the positive luxury of soft-boiled eggs (hens must lay golden eggs for the London market, judging from the price); and I was then ready for the road, probably much better equipped, gastronomically, than the "Wife of Bath" and the rest of that merry company ever thought of being. Outside the hotel there awaited me, not a slow-going donkey, such as "the Wife" rode, but a softly-purring little English motor car. As we drove through the outskirts of London, the sky lost its city murkiness and cleared to a brilliant China blue with fleecy white clouds scudding over it, and the air was soft and balmy. The Englishman certainly loves his flower garden. The front yard of each little suburban home was a kaleidoscope of color; with pansies, great masses of dark blue lobelia, gay daffodils, wallflowers and many others.

At last we were out of London-town and on the Dover road, famous in song and story, in pictures and plays. I wonder if Chaucer's Canterbury Pilgrims ever came this way, or did they set forth from the Tabard Inn at Southwark, not far from here? Anyway, many pilgrims have gone this route through the centuries, on their way to the Cathedral, to worship at the shrine of Thomas à Becket; and that morning I was one of them.

If there is anything more lovely on God's green earth than the countryside in the south of England, on a bright sunny spring day, I don't know what it is. If you have any poetry or romance in your soul, any knowledge of English history or love for the beautiful, such a day in such surroundings will give you a thrill you have never known before. Everywhere, that morning, the grass was the greenest green imaginable (Ireland excepted, of course), with not a weed to be seen anywhere. They don't even seem to know about our principal crop in England. As we rolled along the broad highway, I began to realize why many people select Kent as the most attractive part of England. The great old English oaks were still bare and the delicate tracery of their branches seemed etched against the blue sky; the poplars, straight and tall, were a lovely russet green (only the buds had come as yet); while the willow, most graceful of trees, had that tender light green that comes only in early spring. The whole country-side was dotted with fruit trees in full blossom; the pear, the cherry and the apple trees were great bouquets of pink and white; certainly there will be God's plenty of fruit this year if signs portend. The hawthorn was just coming into bloom and the red berries still clung to the hedges of holly. Out in the meadows, spring lambs gambolled beside their dams. A brilliant spot of yellow on the hillside was a clump of gorse at the height of its bloom, and all the fields were strewn with millions of tiny English daisies, daffodils and bright yellow buttercups. Even the "dainty little dandelion was smiling on the green," if you can think of the dandelion as "dainty" and "smiling."

Over hill and dale, now through a forest and now over a tiny stream, the road wound through small villages and past great estates. What a lot of history and fiction has been created in this part of old Kent! English literature was almost born along this road when old Geoffrey Chaucer lived here. This is not the Shakespeare country; but it was along here that Falstaff and his merry companions were robbed, and Lear and Cordelia met their deaths. Christopher Marlowe and John Fletcher lived close to Canterbury, and William Caxton, England's first printer, was brought up not far off the road. John Evelyn wrote his diary near here and later, much later, Charles Dickens lived at Gad's Hill hard by; and Alfred Tennyson dwelt for a time only a few miles further on. Keats wrote his *Endymion* in this neighborhood, Rosetti and George Eliot and later Joseph Conrad all came to this tiny part of England to live and write. What wonder that, in imagination, one sees the long pageant of English literary history as one rides the Dover road.

At last, through a break in the trees, I caught my first glimpse of the Cathedral spires and knew we were near the goal of our pilgrimage. The great charm of the town of Canterbury is its age. Some of the remains of the Roman occupation are still to be seen, but primarily this is a cathedral city with the Cathedral as its dominating feature.

If you are interested in the history of Gothic architecture, Canterbury Cathedral is an ideal place to study it. But I had not come to study architecture. I had come to worship at the shrine of the martyred saint, Thomas à Becket, thinking that a miracle might be performed for me, as the Canterbury Pilgrims did, and then I would have a Tale to tell. But, alas! When I arrived at the outer door of the crypt, where X marked the spot where the good man was murdered, it was closed for repairs and I could go no nearer.

One view of the interior of the Cathedral I shall always remember. It is looking down a long aisle, with great stone pillars on one side, forming arches eighty feet above and then melting into the groined ceiling. Across the nave the sun was shining through a huge bank of stained glass windows, whose rich colors have been reflected some seven hundred odd years. And as the slanting bars of jeweled sunlight struck the gray pillars, mellowed by time, I thought nothing could be more divinely beautiful.

As one stands on the steps of the transept, drinking in the beauty of the great nave, its gigantic loveliness is fairly overpowering. Certainly, in the centuries during the creation of this building, art was religion and religion was art.

Outside, in the Cathedral close, I stole into what I thought was the Archbishop's garden, to take a picture of the great tower, old Bell Harry, through the flowering branches of a knarled old pear tree. Afterward, I learned that the Archbishops have not been living in Canterbury for several centuries, so I was probably trespassing only in the Dean's garden.

Then came lunch-time, and in strolling down the main street of the town in search of a place to eat, I came to the old Falstaff Inn. It looked so typically early English, with its half-timbered and plastered walls and many-gabled roof, that I could not resist entering. Inside the ceilings were low and the floors slanted at various angles.

"How old is this Inn?" I asked the rotund host who might well have stepped out of a page of Dickens. He was, in fact, almost the personification of Mr. Pickwick himself.

"About five hundred years," he replied, as he drew me a tankard of good old English ale.

Think of it! This place was two centuries old when Shakespeare came this way to gather local color for his plays. Maybe Sir John Falstaff and Prince Hal, themselves, had "quaffed their ale" in the very room where I was having mine. At any rate, what interesting stories of the long ago could the good Falstaff Inn relate if its walls could but speak.

Before I left Canterbury, I wandered up a hillside to old St. Martins, originally built by the Romans before the Cathedral was ever thought of, and from there viewed once more the spires of Canterbury Cathedral through the trees as they rose above the quaint old town.

Then the long ride back to London in the late afternoon, and, as the shadows lengthened from the great oaks that lined the broad highway, thoughts of England and the English people came trooping through my mind. What a troubled outlook this brave little island has had to face ever since the day she entered the World War!

First, the loss of millions of her young men and nothing left to show for the loss but a huge debt which she is unable to pay. While England fought to "save the world for Democracy," Japan was grabbing her trade with the Orient.

Then followed the trouble with Gandhi, which caused a precarious situation in India. Good King George V died and left the throne to an idolized prince, only to have him abdicate at an unpropitious time. In the meantime came strained relations with Italy as the Ethiopian war started and only a short time ago, Germany took over Austria and made a threat to do likewise with Czechoslovakia, which would badly upset the balance of power for all Europe. There is civil war in Spain. Russia, Italy and Germany are building up great fighting machines, their dictators apparently hunting for trouble at any cost. Communism, Fascism and Nazism are spreading on every side and France and England are the only great powers left in Europe with democratic forms of government.

England, today, is working feverishly to prepare herself for war but only as a defensive measure. She does not want war. She learned her lesson in the last one, but she is in a precarious position and she knows it. She will do everything possible to prevent war; but driven into a corner she will fight; and in the meantime she will make every effort to protect and defend herself. There England stands today on a live volcano, knowing full well that an explosion may occur at any time.

Does she tremble in fear of her future?

Not a bit of it.

As a matter of fact, England is fairly prosperous. Prices are high. People are, on the whole, well employed. And even though taxes are burdensome, the Government is not trying to spend itself into prosperity.

England may be threatened by perils from all sides but she has her feet planted more firmly on the ground than any other big power of the world.

Down in South Africa, a man, even though he has been born and spent all his life on the Dark Continent, if he be of English ancestry, always speaks of "going home" to England. That's loyalty! Whether it be in England, in Australia, or in far off South Africa, at the end of every theater performance or public gathering of any kind, the Englishman always rises and stands at attention while the orchestra or band plays *God Save the King*. That's patriotism! And that one act signifies the everlasting love and reverence these people have for their country.

* * * * *

One more sea voyage, the one back to America, and the long eventful trip would be over. One looks for rough weather in January but expects smoother seas in April. However this was not to be and coming home, on the great "Europa," we ran into a hurricane, which furnished the final thrill of an eventful trip.

"Home is the sailor, home from sea
And the hunter home from the hill."

And so back home at last, and one more of life's ambitions has been gratified, one more dream has at last, long last, come true. And in the end let me say that of all the countries I have seen on this fair earth of ours, the lure of South Africa is the strongest.

IX

The Little Virgin Mother

THREE HUNDRED YEARS is a long time ago here in our western world, but it was back in those days that the Catholic missionaries of the Church of Rome, following the Conquistadores across the Andes, with sword in one hand and cross in the other, established the Christian religion all over the La Plata basin, in Argentina, with a hold so strong that it will, in all probability, never be broken.

For many years I have been travelling over Latin-American countries, all the way from Mexico to Patagonia and to me, in these old Spanish towns, the churches and the cathedrals, which invariably constitute the center of interest in each community, are features of greatest charm. Sometimes the buildings are beautiful pieces of architecture or, maybe, there is some interesting tradition in connection with the church's history, but always there is the inspiring sight of the faithful parishioners coming to offer their humble and sincere devotions.

And so it happened that when we came to Buenos Aires and I heard of Lujan, a place of pilgrimage for devout Catholics since 1630, with its beautiful Cathedral erected in honor of the Virgin in the very early days of the country, I determined to make my pilgrimage there.

The town of Lujan (pronounced Lu-han) lies about seventy kilometers west of Buenos Aires. It is in a rich agricultural district and can be reached by motor car over good roads in about two hours. We arrived in this little Spanish town, with its low plaster-covered buildings and narrow streets, about noon. We had been motoring since early morning, and as it was a hot summer day, the small second-class hotel, on a narrow side street seemed inviting, with its dark coolness, in spite of the dirt and the dinginess of its interior. The meal was the usual heavy Argentine lunch of many courses, which should be followed, according to custom, by a siesta. But today we had no time to waste with such a custom, but set out immediately for the thing we had come to see.

In the heart of the town was the inevitable Plaza, drenched in mid-day sunshine, and in the center of the Plaza, as always, an equestrian statue of either San Martin, Bolivar or Belgrano, I have forgotten which. One gets to betting with his companions as to which one of these statues it will be in the next town, with an even chance of winning. Facing this public park was the most beautiful cathedral in all Argentina. It completely dominated the town, with its massive bulk, its flying buttresses and its tall twin spires, just as the little English towns are dominated by their great cathedrals.

As I have said, it was the siesta hour and even the little booths outside, by the entrance steps, where devotional candles of all sizes and colors were sold, were deserted. Inside the church it was dark and cool and restful, a place where the quiet dignity of perfect surroundings inspired deep religious feeling.

Instead of the ornate interior of the overdone Cathedral of Buenos Aires, Lujan is grand in its simplicity. Down the high central nave run great, grey stone columns with carving only at their tops just before they melt into the vaulted and groined

89

ceiling, high above. The stained glass windows are lovely and their coloring is enhanced by the plain gray stone work which surrounds them. Back of the high altar is the small Lady Chapel. In the center of the altar wall, in a small opening, is a beautiful little effigy, about eighteen inches high, of the Virgin Mother, dressed in brilliant robes set with precious stones. At her back is the blue vault of Heaven, from which descend the silver rays of the sun. She is placed on a pivot so that she may look down upon a small gathering in the chapel or be turned to face the main altar in the body of the Cathedral, as the occasion needs. It was in the chapel, as the little Madonna faced us from her place in the wall, that the sacristan told me the following story of how she came to Lujan.

A great many years ago, when the Argentine was much younger than it is now, vessels arriving from Spain, the mother country, were anchored far out in the Rio de la Plata, as there was no harbor at Buenos Aires and the goods arriving had to be lightered to shore in small boats. One day there arrived a cargo of goods destined for one of the great estancias, far up in the pampas country to the west. The boxes and bales were safely transported to shore and there loaded onto a great four-ox-team cart, which was the only means of transportation in those days, and is still used, to a large extent, all over South America. But the roads were wretched in early times and during the rainy season these great carts, with wheels eight feet high and drawn by four or six slow-going but powerful oxen, had difficulty in getting through the deep mud of the rich soil of the country.

The consignment started on the long, slow journey to its destination in the up country, but it was the rainy season and the black mud was deep and the going was slow, indeed. After some days of tedious travel the cart arrived at the little village of Lujan and there, in the center of the town, the wheels sank, with a groan, to their hubs in the rich black mud, and the oxen could not budge it an inch further. Down from his seat climbed the

90

patient driver and slowly, box by box, and bundle by bundle, the burden of the cart was lightened — yet still the oxen could not move it! More of the load was taken down until, finally, nothing was left but one small box, not more than two feet square. The oxen strained again but to no purpose; the cart still could not be moved. Then the last small box was lifted down, the oxen lashed and lo! the cart moved forward.

Something strange about this — why should this last small parcel, whose weight was so trifling, make such a difference? The curious villagers gathered about, eyes staring. The box was opened and there, inside, resting on a velvet cushion was a lovely little Madonna, who had traveled all the way from Spain to grace the private altar of some great estanciero who, in his distant home had remained ever true to his faith. Now all of the boxes and bales, save the box of the Little Madonna, which the villagers refused to give up, were reloaded onto the cart and behold! the oxen pulled the great load out of the mud with ease. Here, then, was a direct sign from Heaven. The little Madonna, by some miracle, had known that she had arrived at the very place where she was most needed, to be an inspiration for these simple people, these villagers of Lujan. By some divine insight, she had refused to be taken further on.

Overjoyed by this miracle — wrought before their very eyes — the peasants vowed that the little Mother should go no further but that she should stay in Lujan and they would build for her a great Cathedral, to do her honor. Years went by, and stone by stone, the great building rose and gradually neared completion. Finally the great day came when the magnificent church was finished and the little Virgin Mother, dressed in her brilliant robes, sparkling with jewels, was placed with the utmost reverence in her niche in the altar wall.

For many years now she has looked down from her haven, receiving and answering the prayers, not only of the faithful of Lujan but of her devoted children who come from the country for miles around to kneel before her, and the great Cathedral is known over all of Argentina to this day as the Church of the Little Mother of Lujan.

Outside, again, the sun still blazed down on the Plaza. But the siesta hour was over and the candle women had returned to their booths and the faithful were spending their hard earned pesos for tapers to burn at the feet of the Little Mother, who, in the long ago had refused to leave them, when she knew by divine direction that she had reached her home and her people.

X

Coast to Coast in South America

*I*T WAS always a matter of wonder to me, in my school days, why we were taught so little about South America. Perhaps it is different now, but about all we learned concerning this great sister continent, from which we were severed three decades ago by that great feat of surgical engineering, the Panama Canal, was, that the Brazilian jungles were almost unexplored; that the Amazon was a mighty river; that the Argentine pampas was vast and that the Patagonians were a tall race of people with big feet. Nothing of its interesting history, its beautiful cities or its vast resources. We are going to awaken from our smug self-sufficiency some day, to find that South America has beaten us out of a large part of the world's trade, because we have chosen more or less to ignore her.

If you have a drop of Irish blood in you, you will be more than ever proud of that fact, if you study the history of the west coast of South America. It was in 1817 that a gentleman by the name of O'Higgins — and what name could be more Irish — came over from the old country and started making history for himself and for the west coast. He first liberated Chile and, afterward,

Peru, from the Spanish yoke and initiated many drastic reforms in Chile, which had been frightfully governed under the old Spanish regime. He became the first President of Chile, and today every town in Peru and in Chile has his statue in the main plaza or, at least, the leading hotel is named after him. So in this country of Spanish and Italian names, Hail to O'Higgins, the George Washington of the west coast!

In this chapter, I want to relate how I crossed South America from Valparaiso, on the Pacific or western side to Buenos Aires on the Atlantic or eastern side. There are, or have been, several ways of crossing this vast continent and, then, there is the alternative of sailing around Cape Horn, by way of the Straights of Magellan. This, however, is apt to be a cold and stormy trip and, besides, one would miss the wonderful scenery to be had on any of the other routes.

I think, if I had been a few years earlier, I should have chosen to go by way of the Transandine Railway, but that famous piece of engineering has been out of commission for some years now, as far as crossing the Andes is concerned, for the train at the present time, goes only as far west from Buenos Aires as Mendoza in western Argentina. This used to be the most desirable way to cross the continent, not only because of the grandeur of the scenery in the high Andes but also in order that the traveller might make an arduous side trip to see that world-renowned colossal statue, *The Christ of the Andes*. This statue marks the dividing line between Chile and the Argentine and also commemorates the vow of eternal peace between the two countries, in the following words: "Sooner shall these mountains crumble into dust than the people of Argentina and Chile break the peace to which they have pledged themselves at the feet of Christ the Redeemer." These brave words, however, have since become more or less meaningless, for although the peace has been preserved, the two countries hate each other most thoroughly and have done so for a long time.

94

Then one can fly across the continent, but this is not for me. I am a flyer but not a "high flyer." Perhaps few people realize that next to the Himalayas, the Andes are the highest mountain range in the world and flying at an altitude of twenty-four thousand feet is for younger and bolder and better hearts than mine.

But the best way to cross the country and, perhaps, the latest and most interesting, is by way of the Chilean Lakes and that was the method we chose. This route was only opened to the public a few years ago and when our party crossed, it was still much like pioneering.

The city of Valparaiso, where we left our ship, is a great seaport, the largest on the west coast, south of the equator. It has a fine landlocked harbor and the city rises, tier on tier, up the side of the hills that circle around the bay, and reminds one greatly of our own San Francisco, at least from the boat. One day we spent in driving along the rocky shore for miles; went one evening to the Casino which is almost as fine as the one at Monte Carlo; and, at another time, visited what is said to be the finest hotel in South America, the O'Higgins, of course, and found it to be modernistic to the extreme, and owned, as is nearly everything else in Chile, of a semi-public nature, by the government. "Valpo," as it is commonly called, is a thriving city. It has grown and improved immensely during the last decade, but it is suffering, as is all of Chile, from the after effects of a financial debauch, the money for which came largely from bonds sold to that great sucker country, the United States.

Just preceding our arrival, a great railroad strike of Communists had been going on, but fortunately for us, it was all settled the day before we landed. As we were to travel by rail a great deal in this mountainous country of Chile, the thought that bridges might be blown up just ahead of us, would be decidedly unpleasant.

The railroad journey of ninety-five miles from "Valpo" to Santiago is one of the most enjoyable in all Chile. The parlor coaches were extremely comfortable and the scenery, after bleak and barren northern Chile, was lovely almost beyond description. As the train wound through a rich farming country, you could well imagine yourself in Southern California and, indeed, the latitude is about the same. Many varieties of eucalyptus, weeping willows, locust and tall poplar trees shaded the roads. Corn, alfalfa and rich meadows made for an ideal dairy country and wheat harvest was in full swing. Evidently this locality furnishes Santiago with its fresh food supply, as the well cultivated truck farms seemed to grow every kind of fruit and vegetable known to this part of the world. In the middle distance were low wooded hills in which, apparently, some mining was being done, while in the distance the high snow-covered Andes were purple and blue in the evening twilight. As we climbed a divide, the hills became barren and deserted except for the stately candelabra cactus and herds of white goats. Finally, the railroad wound down the mountain side into the lovely Santiago valley far below. Darkness came on and the lights of Santiago, the capital and largest city of Chile, twinkled in the distance.

This city is ideally situated in a great cup, entirely surrounded by high mountains. At this summer time of the year, darkness did not come until after eight o'clock and the twilight coloring on the mountains was most gorgeous. First they were hazy blue, then as the light failed, a deep purple, and finally a rosy Alpine afterglow. In winter, when there is no haze, and their serrated tops are covered with snow, they must be even more beautiful.

Santiago reminds one a little of Paris. It is well laid out with broad avenues and beautiful parks. The buildings are comparatively low, as in most earthquake countries, but, of recent years, some skyscrapers have been attempted which are miserable failures — as we know skyscrapers. The city is overbuilt and, like the rest of the country, is feeling the effects of the terribly depreciated peso. The shops are mostly very commonplace but a few are excellent.

As I sat on a Park bench one afternoon and studied the people passing by, it seemed to me that they wore cheap and shoddy clothing, and that they all had an inferiority complex in the presence of an American, I mean, of course, a North American. Everything was dirt cheap. I went into the "swankiest" barber shop in town and had a hair cut and shampoo, all for twenty-four cents. If you gave a beggar on the street (and there were many of them) a quarter-cent coin, he would bless you until you were out of sight. The shops kept open until seven-thirty in the evening and people did not start to dine until eight o'clock, but no one was up until nine o'clock in the morning and the stores all closed at noon for two hours. Santiago has grown fast in the last ten years, but its future seems rather uncertain. Its main support is the cattle industry, but don't forget that the chief natural resource of Chile, the nitrate business, is gone and, probably, gone forever. In the United States we are now manufacturing nitrates out of the air cheaper than they can be produced in Chile. Even Chilean copper cannot compete with the mines of Utah.

I cannot see why any young man from the United States would be wise in going to the west coast of South America with the idea of making his fortune.

The most impressive thing about Santiago is the lofty Cerro, or mountain, of San Cristobal, rising a thousand feet above the city. The summit is reached by a cog-wheel railroad and crowning the top is a gigantic statue of the Virgin blessing the city. When lighted by flood lights at night, it can be seen for miles around. From the top of this mountain, there is a fine view of Santiago, now a city of a million population and, truly, the queen city of the western coast.

If you are tempted to visit the Chilean Lake country, don't do it unless you are willing to endure a week of hardships and considerable discomfort. But, on the other hand, you will be repaid a hundredfold with some of the grandest and most glorious

97

IN THE CHILEAN LAKE DISTRICT

scenery that lies out of doors. This region has only been opened to the tourist in the last five years and the railroad travel is hard, the automobile roads miserable and the little hotels most primitive. At least these were the conditions in 1936. No doubt traveling facilities have been improved considerably since that time.

To one who had already seen the Scotch and English lake countries, the Italian lakes and, yes, even those of British Columbia, this region was not anticlimactic. Of course, each lake country has its own peculiar charm, but it seemed to me, that the Chilean lakes had more beauty of color, more wildness and grandeur than any of the others I had seen.

As we motored day after day over these many lakes, in small launches, the whole world seemed blue — blue water, blue mountains and blue sky with billowing white clouds to complete the picture. At times the rugged snow-capped mountains dropping precipitously to the water's edge reminded me vividly of the fjords of Norway. Once we saw a whole mountain of light green ice, part of a great glacier, and, at every turn of our little boat, another snow-crowned range of the high Andes would come into view.

One day we were motoring along a narrow shelf of road near the top of a high mountain, when, suddenly, the driver lost control of the steering wheel and the car swerved to the outer edge of the road. Just as it was about to plunge over the side of the mountain — and at this point it was a sheer drop of about a thousand feet — the front wheels struck a huge rock and the car turned over on its side and hung there! It was a breath-taking moment and nothing but that good old rock prevented us from plunging down that rocky mountain side. Every one climbed out of the upper side of the car in an orderly manner and cameras were at once brought into action.

Pretty good behaviour for a group of tourists who had so narrowly escaped a great catastrophe! One must have a highly developed aesthetic sense, to say the least, to undertake such pioneering.

At the end of the third day, we crossed the border into the Argentine lake district and enjoyed a continuation of the same lofty beauty. On our last day in the lake country our baggage was transferred nine times from launch to motor car and motor car to launch, but it was with real regret that we landed, at last, at beautiful Bariloche, leaving the never-to-be-forgotten Chile and Argentine lake districts behind us as we boarded our train for Buenos Aires.

And now began the most disagreeable of all of our experiences — that of riding for forty hours on a train that has the reputation, from world travelers, of being the dirtiest, and the most uncomfortable train in the whole world, India not excepted. Innocently and happily, we started out on this almost transcontinental train which was to take us all the way to B. A., as the people of Argentine abbreviate Buenos Aires. We saw instantly that our sleeper (torture chamber would be more correct) must have antedated the earliest attempts of Mr. Pullman. It was of all wooden construction, of course, and had wheels that would be more suitable for a baby carriage. Now picture such a train, crowded to capacity, traveling through a hot desert country, the dust blowing in, in clouds, and most of the time NO water for toilet or lavatory purposes, and you have some conception of the hardships of the journey. Beer and wine were plentiful, in the so-called diner, but only with difficulty could we buy a pint bottle of mineral water which we used for brushing our teeth. We had been allowed one small towel, each, for the whole trip. The berths were not made up during the day and the uppers being stationary, we had to crouch over to sit in the lower with no backs but the bare straight sides of the car. This whole railroad journey was a veritable nightmare. Meals were terrible, clouds of dust sifted in and settled over everything and there was almost no porter service to provide any comforts. It was hot, unsanitary and uninteresting and even a continuous game of bridge could not prevent its being the longest forty hours I have ever spent.

I can describe the Argentine country through which we traveled, in a very few lines. After leaving the Argentine Andes you could well believe, for the next twenty-four hours, that you were crossing the most uninteresting part of the Arizona desert, only that here there are no mountains in the distance to break the monotony and the country is apparently absolute waste. A few low bushes; here and there skeletons of animals bleaching in the sun; and, occasionally, a lone ostrich trotting off in the distance, was all that we saw.

No other signs of life!

Toward evening of the second day, we reached Patagonia and there the country resembled western Kansas after a hard dry year. This was the Argentine pampas, of which I had heard so much. On the third day, the country became more fertile and interesting. Small groves of trees appeared, a fair corn crop was ripening and fat cattle and horses were much in evidence. It was apparently a dairying country and might well have been central Kansas at its best.

As the train neared Buenos Aires the land became very rich and prosperous looking farm buildings were everywhere. We had come, at last, to the fine agricultural district that surrounds this great city and we began to realize that eastern Argentine is destined to be one of the great crop and cattle producing countries of the world.

Buenos Aires has a population of about two and a half million people, the second largest Latin city in the world, and, like Santiago, in a great many ways also reminds one of Paris. Unlike many other great cities, during these depression years, it is, by no means statical but great improvements are going on everywhere to make it, eventually, one of the show places of the world. Whole blocks in the downtown areas are being razed, streets widened and parks and circles created, all to beautify the congested business districts. When it comes to parks, playgrounds, athletic fields, botanical and zoological gardens, beaches and amusement parks, I believe there is not the equal of Buenos Aires anywhere.

Certainly the people of this city know how to play during their spare time, and now that the whole country is prosperous, they take plenty of time to amuse and enjoy themselves. We happened to be there during carnival week, the week preceding Lent, and men, women and children were giving over the whole week, day and night, especially the night, to having a good time. Shops were closed most of the day and business was at a standstill.

One Sunday we went to the races. It is well known that these people are mad about horse-racing and Buenos Aires has, next to Paris, the finest race course in the world. During the afternoon I placed a bet on a horse — only a few pesos — promptly forgot about it and went down to the quarter stretch rail to take a "movie" of the finish. There were sixteen horses in the race and what was my astonishment to see my choice nose out the favorite and come in first, to win. And so a little of Argentina's wealth came to Kansas and I have the pictures to show how it happened.

It is true that the South Americans are great gamblers; it seems to be inherent in their Spanish blood. But let this be said to their everlasting credit, that a large percentage of the profits of all forms of gambling, whether it be horse-racing, lotteries or roulette, goes to the government, to be used for the support of all charitable and benevolent institutions, so that when one gambles, whether he wins or loses there is the righteous feeling that one is helping in the support of some good cause.

There are buildings of every type in Buenos Aires and few distinctively Spanish or South American in architecture. Many apartment houses then under construction were of the most modernistic type. Avenues and boulevards are exceedingly broad, with long lines of fine trees that extend for miles and miles. Some of the public buildings would do credit to any city in the world and the monuments and statuary in the parks and plazas almost outdo Rome, in quantity if not in quality.

From the windows of our room, high up in the City Hotel, we had an excellent view of this great city. In the middle foreground flowed the broad Rio de la Plata, one of the great rivers of the continent, and a perfect harbor for the many ships that come from every corner of the maritime world. Along the water front of the La Plata runs the Balnearia, the Riverside Drive of Buenos Aires, a favorite place for the fashionable to drive and promenade, and from this broad boulevard there is a fine view of the bathing beaches and the shipping.

As we sailed down the La Plata for Uruguay and left Buenos Aires and the trip across the continent behind us, we turned to look once more at this great city which has come into being during the last half century. It is hard to believe that only fifty years ago its present site was nothing but a mud flat. Today Buenos Aires, with its many styles of architecture, from the historic Cabildo to the most modernistic apartment houses and office buildings; with its lovely Cathedral, its Art Galleries, museums, zoological gardens, parks and playgrounds is truly the wonder city of all South America.

STATUE OF PRIMITIVE URUGUAYAN, MONTEVIDEO

XI

I Dine with A President

*S*OUNDS impossible for a lowly Kansan!

Yes and without political prestige or even a letter of introduction. However, that is exactly the experience I had in Montevideo, Uruguay, in the winter of 1936. It all came about at the lovely Hotel Carrasco on the beach, just out of town.

The rest of the party had all donned their bathing suits and gone to the ocean for a swim but I remained behind to photograph the fine statuary around the lawns of the hotel, and had then gone to the hotel bar room for repairs. As I sat waiting for lunch time and my party to return, I fell into conversation with a gentleman who proved to be the big banker of Montevideo. We found much of common interest to talk about and finally, he, with true South American hospitality, said, "The President of Uruguay is giving a dinner here today in honor of the Mayor of Buenos Aires. I am sure he would be happy to have an American guest. Will you come?"

Would I come!

I would give a year of my life to come — not only to meet these dignitaries but to get something on the rest of my party,

BRONZE "PIONEER" MONUMENT, MONTEVIDEO

who had deserted me. Fortunately it was a noon luncheon and my white linens were "comme il faut," even in this high society.

Before long the President arrived in a "low-necked" automobile, accompanied by a large escort of mounted police or cavalry men, in brilliant red and blue uniforms and clanking swords. It began to look like storybook stuff to me. Some of the soldiers dismounted and stood around in every corner of the first floor of the hotel, leading to a large dining room overlooking the sea. Others remained outside on horseback standing guard at every approach to the building. Presently the Mayor and the President came down the hall arm in arm, and entered the dining room and the rest of us trailed in humbly behind.

The luncheon guests, about twenty-five in all, were seated around a huge circular table, banked with red and white flowers. The meal started with caviar, served in blocks of ice cut in various fancy designs, and ran on through many courses of perfectly wonderful food, including "crepe Suzettes" which to me are only glorified pancakes, and ended with ices of exotic flavors.

Champagne was served all through the meal until cigars were passed near the end. During the luncheon, as the spirit moved him, some one would arise, of his own volition and offer a toast, which seemed to me a good idea, instead of having a toastmaster. You see I was raised a Quaker.

While the wine was flowing freely, the Mayor of Buenos Aires, with no introduction, arose to his feet (without assistance) and as we might say "tore the bone out" in a flowery speech, chiefly about President Terra. And don't think those people can't do it.

I attended Rotary meetings all over South America and never have I heard better or more dignified speech-making anywhere, and, as I did not understand much Spanish, they always had the courtesy to seat some one who could translate next to me.

Finally the President arose and toasted the fair ladies of Argentina. He did a beautiful job of it and got a big "hand" from the gallant gentlemen around the table. Then those of us who had not already had the opportunity of meeting him were presented to the President. When it came my turn to greet him, I wanted to remark: "Mr. President, I think my country could learn something from the way you have been running things down here in Uruguay, if we are determined to go in for dictatorship as we seem to be". But I refrained, and merely thanked him for the great honor of attending his party.

Then every one arose. The President and the Mayor again locked arms and strolled out of the room, the guards, in their gaudy uniforms following, and the party was over. The officials climbed into their cars; the soldiers mounted their horses; a bugle sounded; a command was given and off they rode in a cloud of dust.

No, boys and girls, the age of romance is not over yet!

Now to us, in this country, the President of Uruguay does not sound like so much, but down there Dr. Gabriel Terra is a "big gun" and he has had a very interesting history, which runs something like this.

Shortly after he was elected president, about seven years ago, he called both houses of the government together, in the capitol building, which, by the way, is about as fine as our own in Washington, perhaps, in many ways, even finer, and made a speech outlining his policies. At the conclusion of the talk, he asked how many were for him and how many were against him. Nearly every member was against him and his reform policies. Uruguayan politics, at that time, were very corrupt and the "statesmen" were a terrible bunch of grafters. So, being a strong man, President Terra, South American-like, had them all arrested and threatened them with confiscation of their property on some pretext or other. Of course, he is a dictator — all South American presidents are. This brought the "statesmen" to time in short order and they have been behind him ever since.

From the time that President Terra took office, the republic has been very prosperous, probably the most prosperous of all

108

the South American countries. Immense savings in the cost of government were almost immediately apparent and a general clean-up in political affairs took place all over Uruguay.

They have balanced their budget every year, (where have I heard that term before?) and have never defaulted on their bonds, something almost unique in South American finance.

Montevideo, the capital and largest city of Uruguay, with a population around eight hundred thousand, is one of the most beautiful cities of that continent and is growing very rapidly. There are good roads everywhere, much better than those in the Argentine. Their chief exports are cattle, sheep, hides and wool, all of which are bringing good prices. Some of the largest packing-houses of the world are in Montevideo. Most of the exports go to England and the European continent but I doubt if you would fail to find Uruguayan canned meat products in any grocery store, of any size, in the United States today. Their climate is said to be almost perfect and from my own observation in my short visit there, the people seemed of a much higher class than anywhere else in South America. There is very little poverty and practically no unemployment.

So now, I give my toast to you, President Terra. "You may be a dictator but you are a darned good one and almost single-handed you have had the backbone and the ability to bring order out of a rotten political and economic situation and the credit of Uruguay's prosperity today goes almost wholly to you!

Salute! May you live long and prosper!"

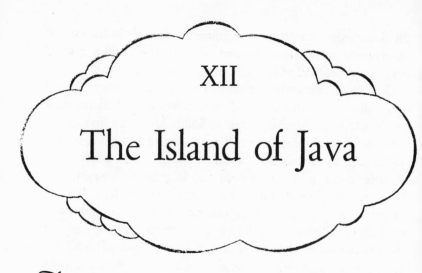

XII

The Island of Java

$\mathcal{D}$URING THE PAST FEW YEARS certain islands in the South Seas have been written about and written about until we are fairly sick of them. First it was Tahiti, and the way this "earthly paradise" was overdone in literature caused it to become commercialized and spoiled in a few years. Then it was Bali, and this beautiful little island is on the way to the same fate, and I suppose, in a few years some other island, if there is any left, will come into favor as "earth's last paradise." I have never been to Tahiti, but, thank goodness, I visited Bali before they began naming restaurants after it in Hollywood.

But Java, just across the straits from Bali—land of the wayang, the batik and the sarong — they will never spoil that island, any more than they will spoil England, by the annual visits of sightseers. There is too much of it, its interests are too diversified, and it has too much individuality of its own, acquired through the centuries of its history, to be influenced by external curiosity. Of the five large islands of the East Indies, namely, Java, Sumatra, Borneo, Celebes and New Guinea; Java will always be much the most interesting to the traveller because of its people and because of its importance in the world's commercial affairs. Its history, its scenery and its immense fertility make it one of the most interesting places in the southern hemisphere.

In the first place, let us definitely locate Java in our minds as to its place on the map. In a general way it lies northwest of Australia and is a part of that string of innumerable islands which extends all the way from the Malay Archipelago on the southeastern tip of Asia to the northwest corner of the continent of Australia, and known as the Dutch East Indies. These islands undoubtedly once formed a connecting link between Asia and Australia, but at some remote time a great disturbance of the earth, in this locality, caused this large body of land to sink into the sea until only the tops of the higher lands remained above the water line to form the most romantic group of islands in the known world.

Our approach to Java was from the east. We had left that wild and woolly cannibal island of Papua, or New Guinea, behind and were sailing westward, day after day, through waters most difficult to navigate. The captain was at his post on the bridge day and night, and, although the weather was fine, there were islands and shoals continuously, first through Torres Strait where we again sighted the northern tip of Australia, and then into the Arafura Sea. Passing the island of Timor on our left, we entered the Banda Sea. We were in a regular trade route now, and ships were continually passing headed east for Australia and South America. Next we passed into the Flores Sea with Celebes to the north and Flores on the south, and innumerable small islands, mostly atolls, on every hand. We were sailing almost straight west and about four hundred miles south of the equator; the weather was fine and cool, and life on deck delightful.

Finally the Java Sea was entered and, as we continued westward, the large island of Borneo was to the north, but we wound slightly southward past the island of Madura, and finally sighted the intoxicatingly beautiful little island of Bali and anchored

111

on her lea side in the Indian Ocean. Verily we had sailed the Seven Seas!

Another twenty-four hours of sailing, and we arrived at our first port in Java, Samarang, but before landing, let us stop to review, briefly, the history of this tropic Eden of the glamorous East. Long before Britannia ruled the waves, Spain and Portugal were sailing the seven seas and claimed all that part of the world by right of discovery. But the defeat of the Spanish Armada put English ships in the Far East as a consequence, and Sir Francis Drake's voyage to the East in 1588 in search of the spice trade resulted, eventually, in the forming of the British and Dutch East India Companies, which were to fight for supremacy in this part of the world for the next two hundred years. Both companies settled in Java at a location where Batavia now stands, but eventually Dutch thrift won out over the English enterprise, as the British insisted on paying out their immense profits in dividends, while the Dutch kept theirs in Java, as a surplus fund as it were, to build and strengthen their position.

In 1641 the Dutch took most of the Malay Peninsula from the Portuguese; the English were economically driven out of the East Indies, and the Hollanders were left to absolute domination of all trade beyond India for a long while. No one travels in this part of the world today without hearing a great deal about those two great Englishmen, Francis Light and Stamford Raffles; Light, of course, at Penang in the Malay States, and Raffles, who not only founded that great port, the crossroads of the world, Singapore, but also explored and wrote home about Java. Were it not for him all Malaya would probably be Dutch colonies today. Raffles' time was during the Napoleonic wars, and he persuaded his government to send a force to Java to fight for its possession. The English defeated the combined Dutch and French forces then holding Java, and Raffles himself was appointed Governor. This remarkable man ruled well, instituting many reforms, but was not given long to serve, for Java was handed back to Holland in 1816 by a treaty designed to secure Dutch good will in Europe. So Java has been Dutch ever since. And right well do they govern it today, if the judgment of a casual observer like myself is of any value. I believe there is less crime among these forty odd millions of happy people in a year that there would be in the city of Chicago in a month.

But let's get back to Samarang, a typical tropical seaport town, where automobiles were awaiting to take us inland.

Did you ever wonder what became of all the old automobiles? I did — until I went to the South Seas, and there I found all my old time friends, even to the curved dash Oldsmobile which merrily rolled along at home at the beginning of the century. In such a car, then, we left Samarang to start on a wild ride into the mountains.

The Javanese boys are the worst chauffeurs in the world. They seem to have no sense of caution and no brakes on their cars. We were in two wrecks in one day and narrowly averted several others. However, the roads are generally fine and the scenery so varied and beautiful that we forgot to be nervous about the driving.

As we leave the seacoast and begin to ascend to the higher ground of the interior on our way to visit the Boroboedoer, one of the most famous Buddhist temples in the world, let us digress a moment to consider this island as a whole. Java is approximately the same size as England without Wales — about fifty thousand square miles in area, and has a larger population, some forty-one million, against England's thirty-six million. It is the most thickly populated country on earth, there being approximately eight hundred people to the square mile. But this is a strictly agricultural country, and there is no feeling of crowding as we know crowds in our western world. The natives are evenly distributed among the fertile fields and hills and valleys in which they toil so unceasingly. Nature has been good to them, the soil is unbelievably rich, everything grows luxuriantly, and the peo-

113

ple are a peaceful, happy lot in this quiet, restful place, far from the noisy, nerve-racking modern world.

As we wound along the shady roads, the little native huts behind their bamboo fences peeped out at us through the thick foliage. We were never out of the sight of people; they were everywhere, a good-looking, good-natured lot with a cheery word of welcome as we sped along through village and countryside. The children were especially enthusiastic about our visit, and, to hear a group of them cheer, as we whirled by, we thought they must be mistaking us for the Queen of Holland.

Java is the "home" of Batik, and as we in America have become Batik conscious, only during the past few years, perhaps a description of how it is made would be of interest. Batik making is all done by hand, usually on cotton cloth but sometimes on silk which is worn only by the upper class. First, the cloth is covered with a design in wax which is traced on by the use of a tiny "teapot" kept heated so that the wax will flow from the spout. It is then dipped in a dye of the desired color, the wax, of course, protecting certain parts of the cloth from the dye. After drying, the wax is then dissolved by acid, the cloth dried, and it is then ready for another design on the protected and undyed portion. This is done a second time, the already dyed portions being protected by wax, and again the cloth is dipped in dye of another color. This process may go on and on until the design more or less elaborate, is completed. It is a slow, tedious business, but to the people who do it, time is no object and it has never been commercialized. The results are beautiful; no two designs are ever alike, and the colors made from vegetable dyes are soft and harmonious.

Javanese people adore color, and the "Sarong," the universal and perhaps only garment of men, women and children, is of all colors of the rainbow and usually made of Batik. These people have a mania for cleanliness, and are forever washing themselves and their garments, always in public, by the way, with no thought of immodesty, and were it not for their disgusting habit of betel-nut chewing they would be the most beautiful and picturesque people it has ever been my lot to see. The farm houses are gathered together in little groups or "Kampongs" as they are called, and each tiny thatched hut has its vegetable and flower garden, the latter a riot of color with tropical blooms.

Incidentally, the women do most of the work in this man's paradise. They labor in the fields and in the home. They predominate in the market place and outnumber the men everywhere. It pays to be born a boy in Java, for the male child is given every care while the female child is left to shift for herself. For some unknown biological reason there are seven girl babies born to every three boys, and so no wonder men are at a premium and truly appreciated.

The women, with their erect carriage and beautiful brown skins, bare from the waist up, are really the backbone of the country. The man as a rule is an inferior being whose chief ambition in life is to own a couple of game cocks upon whose prowess he is willing to wager his wife's earnings. My most vivid impressions of the innumerable kampongs we passed through were the large wicker cages of game cocks set outside each door, the little bunches of rice heads drying in the sun near the doorstep, and the ever-present group of children cheering us welcome; and in the country, everywhere, the rice fields, the most picturesque of growing crops, with tier on tier of small irregular patches in all stages of cultivation.

About noon of this first day, we arrived at the famous Boroboedoer. This truly wonderful Buddhist temple, a relic of bygone centuries, is no doubt next in importance to that wonder of wonders, Angkor Wat in Cambodia. In fact, one author has said, "It is the greatest of them all in architectural virtuosity and in its first condition more costly and imposing than the pyramids." The religious history of Java shows that at heart the inhabitants through the ages have been Buddhists, but various conquerors have compelled the people for a time at least to adopt outwardly their own beliefs. The date of the building of this enormous temple is unknown, but it was probably in the sixth or seventh century. Sometime during a Brahman regime the Buddhists covered up the great temple with earth to preserve it from destruction by disbelievers, and so it remained practically unknown through the centuries until Raffles' time when it was unearthed in all its marvelous beauty. The Boroboedoer is a huge, four-sided truncated stone pyramid, an enormous cap over the top of a low hill. On its summit is a great stone Buddha, and along its sides are four hundred lesser Buddhas, each in a niche or small shrine of its own. But the most remarkable thing about this great temple, which is nearly a mile around its base, is the thousands of elaborate low relief carvings running around the galleries at various levels. These carvings are exceedingly well done and depict the history of ancient times in the eastern world. Some represent the pre-birth life of Buddha, others his descent to earth to teach, and still others the five disciples who wandered with him during his early years. One could spend weeks in studying them and their meanings.

In the late afternoon our road led us higher and ever higher, for we were to spend the night in the cool mountain town of Djokjakarta. Arriving in "Djokja," as it is commonly called, we found it like all other Javanese towns, exceedingly Dutch. Our hotel was very comfortable, and it was here, the next morning, that I had my first experience with a Javanese bath. The bathroom consists of a small stone cubicle in which one strips and stands as though for a shower bath, but instead, an attendant, usually a native girl, stands on a step above and ladles over you cold water from a great gourd which she replenishes from a tank nearby. It's a Spartan experience, but, my! how invigorating after a hot day or night!

It was also at this hotel that I first made the acquaintance of a "Dutch wife," so universally known and used in the East Indies.

It consists of an oblong sawdust pillow, or bolster, which lies across the bed and presents a hard, cool surface on a sweltering night. By throwing an arm and leg over the pillow the air is allowed to circulate freely between the limbs, assuring comfortable slumber, thereby making an ideal sleeping companion. Anywhere you travel in this part of the world, you are sure to find a "Dutch wife" reposing on your bed.

As I was wandering about town toward nightfall, I became conscious of weird music being played on instruments, the like of which I had never heard before. Following the sound I was led back to our own hotel where I found a "wayang" show in progress. A wayang is a shadow show in which the figures in silhouette are thrown on a screen by a light from behind. It is somewhat like a marionette show only all the puppets are operated by one person. No words are spoken; it is purely pantomime accompanied by an orchestra which makes the strangest music imaginable. This primitive sort of orchestra is called a "gamelan," and consists mainly of a series of different-toned gongs and an instrument made of various lengths of hollow bamboo, known as an "anklong" which, when struck, gives forth a weird and melodious sound. The wayang, and the accompanying gamelan, are used at all first class weddings and other festive occasions. No one who has been to Java will ever forget them. As a matter of fact, the puppet show originated in Java, and so long ago that its origin is unknown.

Our second day's travel was from Djokjakarta to the little mountain town of Garoet, all the way by train, and a surprisingly good train it was, equipped with what looked like an American engine and fairly comfortable cars. This day's travel led us through the richest agricultural part of the island, and as there was a very intelligent and communicative native in the car, a veritable riding Javanese encyclopaedia, this is a good place to give you some of the information I gleaned from him during the day, plus the observations I made from the car window.

117

If you are a volcano "fan," you should go to Java, for there are more volcanoes there, both active and inactive, per square mile than anywhere else on the globe. I believe there are about a hundred more or less active ones on the island, and you are scarcely ever out of sight of a smoking cone. This may not sound reassuring, but it is the secret of Java's having the most productive soil to be found anywhere: a rich, volcanic soil which coupled with plenty of rain and sunshine will grow many things that simply won't grow anywhere else on earth.

Take cinchona for instance. First discovered in South America by the Spaniards, it was in danger of becoming extinct, as gathering the bark killed the tree, but it was discovered that the tree, which yields that invaluable alkaloid quinine, could best be cultivated in Java, and today the total production on this island is about eighteen million pounds weight per year, or about ninety-five percent of the world's consumption. The trees can only be grown at an elevation of about five thousand feet, and we saw numerous groves of the cultivated trees from the train.

Rice, of course, is the staff of life in Java, as it is nearly everywhere in the Far East. There are twelve thousand square miles of it grown here, and it is practically a continuous crop the year round, but in spite of this immense production it is necessary to import more rice to feed this enormous population. Being a loyal Kansan, I still think there is nothing more beautiful in nature than a golden wheat field rippling and waving in the breeze, but certainly a rice field in almost any stage of cultivation is most picturesque. These little fields may be of any size and shape, but usually they are small, curving shelves rising tier above tier on the mountain side, and all, of course, watered by an elaborate system of irrigation, which will be spoken of later. As I have said, it is a continuous crop, as Java is a land of springtime and summer the year round. In one view you may see this crop in all stages of cultivation; the plowing of the muddy soil with a crude plow drawn by the fierce water buffalo; the planting of the small pale green shoots — a backbreaking job — always done by women, for otherwise the Javanese believe the rice will not be fruitful; the growing young plants turning the field to a vivid emerald green; and finally the ripening grain, making a carpet of golden heads, somewhat resembling a Kansas wheat field. Through all these stages the little fields are thronged with natives in their bright-colored sarongs, plowing, planting, weeding, and finally gathering the ripened yellow heads by hand. When the rice begins to ripen the birds descend on it in great numbers to feed. To combat this a bamboo platform is placed in the middle of the field, and cords, garnished with rags and bits of paper, are strung from its posts to others at the edges of the "sawah" or field. All day long children, stationed on a central platform, jerk these cords to frighten off the greedy birds until the grain is safely harvested.

I have mentioned the subject of irrigation. To think of Java without irrigation is impossible. It is its lifeblood, and everything in the island, its romance, its charm, its very wealth and civilization, is dependent upon it, for without it Java would be another wilderness like New Guinea or Borneo, and peopled only by a few primitive savages. This illustrates very well, I think, that water, properly applied, can turn a sparsely inhabited wilderness into a land supporting the densest population in the world. How long this elaborate system of watering the mountain sides has been in existence no one knows, but probably for thousands of years, and to think of irrigation in Java is to think of rice, for it was to grow his staple food that the Javanese farmer first harnessed the streams and became an irrigator. Modern irrigation dates back to early in the 18th century, but the Dutch government took it over in 1854 in order to increase the production of rice to feed the rapidly multiplying population. Mostly the water is led in its devious courses through small ditches, but there are miles and miles of bamboo piping and rickety-looking aqueducts made of hollow tree trunks resting upon lanky bamboo supports. As one views this intricate system, it is hard to believe but that they actually make the water run uphill. I don't know that these people have the most scientific irrigation system in the world, but I defy you to show me one more practical.

Perhaps the question has come to your mind, "With what do these people build their houses?" and the answer is, "Out of bamboo." As a matter of fact, the bamboo is about the most important plant grown in Java, for it is put to a multitude of uses. To house forty million people in comfort is undoubtedly the main one. In every man's backyard is a clump of the bamboo, the easiest thing in the world to grow in this climate. To build a house the native merely splits the stems of the plant and weaves them together into sheets called "bilik." These sheets form the walls; large bamboo poles, the framework; and the leaves, the thatch for the roof; and there you are, cheap, strong and easily repaired. This is only one of the many uses of the ubiquitous bamboo. As I have already said, there must be thousands of miles of it in Java's irrigation system. It is used for plumbing in the houses; a section of it for a bucket, and a hundred other household purposes. The long carrying pole or "pickeolan" over the shoulders of a native with a pail on either end, is a most familiar sight on the country roads. Bamboo bridges are a feature of the Javanese landscape. Sometimes these are very elaborate suspension bridges, certainly a triumph of the native skill. Many musical instruments are made of this universal material, among them the "anklong," used as already stated, in the shadow play orchestras. Bamboo is finely split and woven into hats, and this is one of the principal industries of Java. We were later to find out in Bangkok, Siam, that the famous Bangkok hats, so prized in this country, were not made there at all, but in Java, out of the pandanus and bamboo. in fact, one could go on, almost without end, in the uses of this prolific plant.

The Dutch have encouraged the cultivation of European flowers and vegetables of recent years, and so now we find a tiny garden plot in every kampong. Here grow, in profusion, in the rich volcanic soil, chrysanthemums of every shade, roses, tiger lilies, azaleas, gladioli, arums, stocks, verbenas, cannas, marigolds, sunflowers, irises and a hundred others. In the vegetable garden, are rows of cabbages, lettuce, carrots, leeks, onions, peas, beans, spinach, tomatoes, beets and what not.

I wish I could give you some idea of the delicious fruits of Java. Most of them, aside from the banana, I had never heard of before, and my palate was treated to some entirely new and delightful sensations. Perhaps the best known is the mangosteen. A taste for most exotic fruits is an acquired one, but everyone seems to like the mangosteen from the first. It is said that the Queen of Holland has offered a million dollars for a sample of this fruit peculiar to this colony of hers, delivered to her table, and yet she has never tasted it because of its perishableness in transport. So you may never know the joy of eating a mangosteen unless you make a trip to the Dutch East Indies. Then there is the rambutan, somewhat similar to the mangosteen; the mango, native to the whole of the East Indies; the sapodilla and the granidilla, with their delicate flavors; the breadfruit and jackfruit; and last, but by no means least, is the papaya, which we had grown fond of in Honolulu and which is now being cultivated even in Southern California.

But enough, for awhile, of the apparently limitless plant life of this teeming country through which we had been travelling most of the day. In late afternoon we arrived at the small mountain town of Garoet in the heart of volcano land. Our little Dutch hotel was spotlessly clean, cool and comfortable, but towards evening we noticed numerous little brown and green lizards three or four inches long running about the ceiling. I asked the native boy attendant to do something about it, but he smiled indulgently and informed me that they were only tjik-tjak. I found out afterward that these lizards are almost a domestic animal; that they sleep by day and run about the walls and ceiling of your bedroom at night catching mosquitoes and other noxious insects. The name comes from a little sound he gives when hunting is good. We heard these little fellows running about all night long; occasionally one would lose his footing and fall with a soft "plop," but the beds were covered with mosquito netting so none fell on our faces, but nevertheless it was rather an unrestful night.

The next morning before leaving I went to see the Dutch landlady about having a traveller's check cashed for some pocket money. What was my surprise when she said, "Nothing doing, your old United States exchange is so uncertain nowadays, you don't know what it's going to be worth by the time you get it to the bank." In all my travels in many foreign countries, this was the first time Uncle Sam's money was not at least at par. Since we went off the gold standard, foreign exchange has been doing some funny things, and this same cruise for the following year had to be abandoned on account of the uncertainty of the exchange rates.

Our third day's trip was by automobile again, and leaving Garoet, on the high table lands, we gradually descended all day through various climatic gradations until in the evening we reached the tropical city of Batavia, on the coast. During this beautiful and exciting drive, and I say exciting because these native boys were absolutely irresponsible chauffeurs and continually kept us guessing, we were again impressed with the diversity of crops which is possible in a country where nature has been so kind.

Tobacco is grown in Java, but only in limited areas, about twenty-five thousand acres in all, and although the quality is good for wrapping and filling cigars, the Javanese tobacco cannot compare with that grown on the neighboring island of Sumatra, and besides the cultivation of this crop is so depleting to the soil that it must lie fallow for seven years between crops. Cassava, which yields that product familiarly known to us as tapioca, is quite extensively grown in Java, and the country exports some two hundred and fifty million pounds of it annually. It is an easy crop to grow, does not require much water, and its yield is six times as great as an acre of wheat.

A scraggy looking tree often seen along the roadside is the "Kapok." This tree bears large pods which contain a soft, silky "tree cotton." It is almost peculiar to Java, and the product is valuable, because of its extreme lightness, for filling mattresses, pillows and cushions, and is used throughout the world for life-saving apparatus.

Of course, when we think of Java, we think of coffee, and at one time this island was the world's largest producer, but it has yielded the palm to South America, and Brazil is now in the lead, with Java in third place.

As in all tropical countries, there is an immense number of coconut palms, and a large quantity of copra is exported.

"Citronella" is another interesting Java crop. It is used as the base for the manufacture of perfume, although you probably know it as a mosquito bite preventative.

Coca, from which we get the valuable alkaloid, cocaine, is cultivated in Java, as is also the vanilla bean. In fact, when you get into drugs and spices, you can run pretty well through the entire list of the Pharmacopoeia.

Maize is largely grown, roughly about four million acres of it, as are also soy beans and sisal hemp to further diversify the crops.

The Javanese have a clever faculty of utilizing all the fertile ground possible for some useful and productive purpose. There are large areas of swampy land near the coast now devoted to the cultivation of cane sugar, and Java is today second only to Cuba in the production of the entire supply, producing one-fifth of the world's consumption. This may sound like an exaggeration, but my authority is a high one, and as this is being written in California, superlatives are to be expected. The raising of cane sugar has done more to develop the country than any

123

other crop or industry. It has built roads, bridges, railroads, canals, schoolhouses, hospitals, and over a hundred sugar mills. Well may they say, "In Java, Sugar is King!"

I must speak of one more crop before I leave agriculture. Rubber! Before the world's slump this was one of the island's most profitable crops, and there are still about a thousand rubber estates in Java, but they are only marking time, now, until prices get better, and are cultivating other crops between the rows of rubber trees to help out, in the meantime. Unlike the Malay Peninsula, which we were to visit later, where rubber is the main crop, the temporary eclipse of the rubber industry has not hurt Java where crops are so diversified. At that, Java and the other islands of the Dutch East Indies are furnishing thirty-five percent of the world's rubber supply.

The Chinese are a very significant factor in Javanese life. They are energetically engaged here, as elsewhere in the Orient, in industrial, commercial and agricultural activities. They are bankers, farmers, storekeepers, owners of sugar mills, and play a large part in every activity of the country.

On the way to Batavia, we spent an hour in the modern Dutch town of Bandung, with its beautiful residences, lawns, and gardens of apparently every known cultivated flower and tree. We had stopped for an interesting visit at a tea factory, where most of the work was done by hand by native women, and had lunched on native dishes and fruits on the wide veranda of a mountain hotel. Toward mid-afternoon we came to Buitzenzorg, known the world over as, perhaps, the finest botanical gardens in existence. Whether this is true or not, certainly it is in the front rank, with its wide vistas of magnificent tropical trees of infinite varieties, its placid lakes and acres of gorgeous flower beds. One large slat house is entirely devoted to the cultivation of orchids, which alone to the flower lover is worth the trip to Java.

From Buitenzorg the road winds slowly down to that well known coastal city of Batavia, which was to be the end of our

Javanese journey. As we approached Batavia, the road widened to a boulevard flanked on one side by great "godowns" or warehouses, and on the other by a wide canal, the main artery of the city, upon which were innumerable rafts ladened with all sorts of products on the way to market, and propelled by colorful natives with long bamboo poles.

Batavia, with a population of about one hundred and fifty thousand, is the capital and chief city of the Dutch East Indies. It is a combination of a very old native town and a beautiful modern Dutch city, with luxurious gardens and choice tropical plants. It is the principal seaport, and from here are shipped most of the exports on their way to Singapore, the clearing house of the Orient. Three of the great sources of natural wealth on this bountiful island are the dairy industry, the vast teak wood forests, and the great tea plantations; whereas in the British East Indian colonies, one is dependent on canned condensed milk, in the Dutch colony of Java pasteurized milk may be had everywhere. Which brings me to the point that the Dutch are model colonizers, and they have succeeded in molding Java into their most successful colony. Here they are dealing with all sorts of people — millions of natives and thousands of Europeans, Chinese, Japanese and Arabs, and although, as already stated, it is the most thickly populated country on earth, the inhabitants all dwell together in peace and harmony, everyone is well fed and contented, and the country has never been so prosperous commercially as it is today.

As we sailed away from this beautiful land, for other ports of call, my most vivid impression of it was the happy peacefulness of these kindly brown people. At no time during our stay had I seen drunkenness or rowdyism of any kind. They seem to be busy and contented, and, living in a land of apparent plenty, there are no extremes of poverty or riches. The kindness of nature seems to be reflected in their attitude toward each other and life in general.

From where I sit writing this paper (near San Diego, California) comes the sound by night and day of the preparation for war, or, perhaps, I should say preparedness against war. The reverberations of big guns on battleships off shore, the drone of hundreds of government seaplanes overhead, and the distant rattle of the gunfire of target practice at a nearby fort are almost constant. I turn to the daily papers and read the news of European countries, all preparing themselves for war as never before. The white races of the world seem to be using most of their time and money thinking of ways to annihilate each other, and we in the United States spend enough each year on our navy alone to feed all the hungry in our land. About one more world war, they say, and civilization as we know it among the white races would be finished for some centuries at least.

Some great writer, Spengler, I believe, has predicted the decline and downfall of the white races and the ultimate predominance of the brown-skinned people of the earth. To us who live in the Middle West, in a peace loving, agricultural country, far from any warlike preparations, this seems like an absurdity. But when one stops to think that the white races of the world seem to have reached a point in their civilization where they are decreasing in numbers for economic and social reasons, and science is constantly inventing new ways for them to annihilate each other, one cannot but wonder if there may not be a strong probability that the brown-skinned people, so immensely in preponderance already, should eventually rule the world, or a great part of it. At least, let me suggest that a visit to the East Indies, with their wealth of productivity, to unfortunate and bedevilled China with its hundreds of millions of population not yet awakened to its potential possibilities, and finally to Japan, whose people are in many ways the smartest on earth, all increasing in numbers and importance, may well cause any thinking person to stop and seriously ask the question, "Who knows but that the white race has seen its day?"

126

My friend, W. A. Shedd, has written of Java as:

THE LAST PARADISE

Enchanted Isle, thou'rt but a bit of star-dust blown
From distant, cosmic space into the Java Sea,
And yet the sorcery of thy loveliness has won
The interest of a world tired of life's mummery.

Thy palm trees lift their fronds in air and send afar
Soft whisperings of days of peace and calm content;
Thy banyan trees stretch out umbrageous arms and stir
Our hearts to thoughts of love by their soft blandishment.

Above thy terraced fields of rice of shimm'ring green
Grim Batoer stands, begirt with clouds, head lifted high,
Amassing Heav'n's refreshing dews for his demesne,
The Isle to render fecund and to beautify.

Sweet music haunts thy dells, and all thy hamlets ring
With vibrant notes from gamelans' rich melody,
While to their strains, in rhythmic, graceful posturing,
Young maidens dance the blissful, happy hours away.

Thy women stalk the lanes, erect, of beauty rare,
Bare-breasted, unashamed, God-loving, fearing none,
Great burdens on their heads as proudly bear
As wears a queen a coronet of jewelled crown.

In every home, at every hearth, small children play
In innocence, with happy childhood's inborn right;
Thy men heed not ambition's fawning flattery,
Nor know the deadening quest for gold, its fateful blight.

O Java, Isle as lovely as the Eden whence
Were driven those who by the artful serpent fell,
Fain would we linger in thy vales, cast off pretense,
Forget life's harrying cares, and LIVE *beneath thy spell.*

A MIDWESTERN HIGH SCHOOL, TOPEKA, KANSAS

XIII
Art—Its Three Dimensions

$\mathcal{S}$OMEONE HAS SAID, "Art is the greatest thing in the world." This sounds like an extravagant statement at first, but when you come to think about it — why isn't it? Of course we must think of art in its broadest sense — painting, sculpture, music, printing, poetry, architecture, the art of producing ceramics, implements, and the art of design — before we can realize that man ever since the dawn of civilization has striven to perpetuate himself by some means of art.

The cave man with his smoky torch tracing sooty figures of his deeds of valor on the stone walls of his home; the Babylonians baking their clay tablets with history written thereon in curious cuneiform letters; the Egyptians building those great monuments of architecture, the pyramids, were all practising a form of art which has been everlasting in its effects on the development of culture in the ages that have followed.

And then to think of Greece, a little country, not larger than a few Kansas counties, and the tremendous influence she has had on civilization for two thousand years. Why? Greek art, of course. Italy will be remembered for her Michelangelo, her

Donatello and her Cellini long after her Caesars are forgotten.

Germany, more and more as time goes on, will be thought of as a country where the great art of printing first saw the light, at least in our western world. France, of course, would be nothing, comparatively speaking, without her art, and so it goes with other countries in their relation to their importance in history.

I never think of artistic little Japan without thinking first of her inherent love of art, or of weird, old China where the making of paper and printing were practiced long before the western world ever dreamed of them. China's dynasties are marked by the progression or retrogression of art through these centuries rather than by their growth or decay through the political machinations of its emperors.

I have said that every civilized country has shown its importance in history by the development of its art. Little England is perhaps an exception to the rule, especially in sculpture. Strange to say, this great country which has done so much for literature has never produced a great master of the chisel.

And so perhaps after all, this was not an extravagant statement, and "Art *is* the greatest thing in the world." At least it has had the profoundest influence on the appreciation of beauty and culture, and has brought man from the beast to whatever degree of progress he may have attained at various periods of our civilization. In a brief discussion of this vast subject, I will touch only a few of the high spots of that particular phase of art which has to do with sculpture and architecture.

Joseph Hudnut in his charming little book on *Modern Sculpture* says, "Sculpture was born before man was allied to the intellectual forces, before science had taught him to observe, analyze or make use of nature. At first there was no difference between architecture and sculpture, but later necessity separated the two arts. Architecture must provide a shelter, sculpture must represent a god." And as civilization progressed, so architecture no longer remained solid and inert, was no longer controlled by pure geometry, but by the shape and disposition of inward spaces and by the requirements of structure.

This to my mind reached its culmination in the feeling of peace and restfulness we experience in visiting the great cathedrals of Europe. "Sculpture," Hudnut goes on to say, "is form giving. It offers us, like architecture, the measure of a world made harmonious with our own spirit. The difference between architecture and sculpture lies not in their intention but in their materials and processes. The sculptor being obliged to represent, finds in nature the materials for his creative effort." The history of sculpture is the story of mankind, and so if we study this art through the ages, we have a very fair idea of world history.

The Egyptians thought to "save their souls" by portraying the great triumphs of their gods and their kings by erecting gigantic pyramids in their honor, building great tombs and obelisks, and carving that mysterious and ageless object, the Sphinx. True that a great deal of Egyptian history has come down to us through the medium of the papyrus scrolls, but these would never have survived had it not been for the everlasting form of architecture which preserved them through many centuries.

I have in my possession a little, rounded clay tablet covered with cuneiform lettering, which dates back to Babylonian times, about 2250 B. C., or four thousand years. It is a work of art, one of thousands that have come down to us, each telling a bit of the life and history of those times so that today we have a pretty fair picture of Babylonia and Assyria through this early form of art, that of carving in clay.

I have never been able to see anything particularly beautiful in Egyptian art. It is stiff and stilted, and makes no attempt beyond telling a story and honoring and commemorating great deeds and great people, but the Pyramids are the first and greatest example of design in three dimensions.

The next great chapter in art is an entirely different one — that of the Greeks. Here for the first time you have "art for art's sake."

The old time Greeks reached a higher state of perfection in a comparatively short space of time in their architecture and sculpture than had ever been dreamed of, and their masterpieces have never since been excelled.

The perfection in architecture seems to have been reached in the creation of the Parthenon. It "set the pace," so to speak, for architects for all time, and what remains of it today is conceded to be the finest piece of building ever created by man's hand.

The exquisite work of Phidias and the perfection of the sculpture of Praxiteles and a host of others who did their creative work during this golden age of art will probably remain forever the ideal of great art.

Archaic Greek sculpture and architecture, which ceased to develop after the fifth century, could not survive the decay of Hellenic religion because, fundamentally, they were religious arts, and when their religion started to disappear, the incentive to reproduce in building and in statue, works to deify their gods, began to disappear also. But still, in the autumn time of Greek art there were produced some of the best known pieces of sculpture of all time. The Laocoon group now to be seen in the Vatican Museum, the Venus of Milos, perhaps the best known piece of sculpture in the world, who has for many years had her "at homes" in the Louvre, and the Apollo Belvedere, also in the Vatican, are a few examples of the work of the last of the great Greek sculptors.

Our next phase in the development in art, of course, concerns the Romans whose history in this regard runs parallel to our American pioneers. The early Romans were too busy trying to conquer the world to be bothered with trivialities such as art. "Leave to the Greek his marble dolls and scrolls of wordy lore," was the way one of their own poets put it. Theirs was the job of conquering and rebuilding the world in less aesthetic ways. But later, and as they grew in wealth and power, they began to turn to the cultivation of the arts of sculpture and architecture with a greater effort than the world had ever known. This makes you think that Mussolini today is trying to make Roman history repeat itself.

Of course, this was a glorious period, especially in architecture, but the day came when the Roman eagle began to fold his wings and, as Lorado Taft expresses it, "Most appropriately, sculpture's final expression was in the form of magnificent burial cases. Yes, Roman art made itself an elaborate coffin, crept in, and pulled down the lid for a good, long sleep — a slumber of a thousand years." And so the Dark Ages settled down on the western world when for century after century the whole of Europe was to know no progress in civilization.

And then came that period of awakening when for four centuries, from 1150 to 1550, what is known as Gothic art was born, the art of the so-called barbarians, and in France in particular the architects, finding their ideals in the Greek and Roman architecture, created those truly glorious monuments, the Gothic cathedrals of France.

To digress for a moment, in a recent discussion the question came up as to what material was best suited for monumental sculpture, both for beauty and lasting qualities. Some thought bronze, some marble, some granite, and others limestone. Of course, bronze should last forever, but it is very expensive for a monument of any size. Marble is beautiful but cold, and will not stand the outdoor climate of this country. Granite is everlasting but very hard to carve, and makes one think of only one thing —a tombstone. Limestone is, after all, the ideal material. It has warmth, carves beautifully, is found in the finest quality in many places in America, and if you don't believe it has lasting qualities, look at the beautiful cathedrals of medieval Europe and England. Some of these were built nearly eight hundred years ago, and all are of limestone, and their most intricate and delicate carvings have withstood the elements all these centuries and are in almost perfect condition today.

133

The Gothic cathedrals were built in small towns, commemorating the rebirth of religion, and were really an effort to create a lovely fairy story in the midst of surroundings so crude and brutal that they offered a means of spiritual escape from the drab world of the past.

Those of us who have been privileged to see the great cathedrals of Chartres, Notre Dame, Amiens, Reims or Rouen in France and those lovely ones scattered over old England, know something of the beauty of the architecture of that period. These churches of the middle ages were distinctive in their high ribbed vaultings with pointed arches, clustered piers and flying buttresses, and all warmed by the finest stained glass windows ever created. On entering one of these cathedrals I have often had the feeling, so beautifully expressed by some great churchman who said, "When the house of God, many-colored as the radiance of precious stones, called me from the cares of the world, I seemed to find myself, as it were, in some strange part of the universe, which was neither wholly of the baseness of the earth nor wholly of the serenity of heaven; but by the grace of God, I seemed lifted in a mystic manner from the lower, toward that upper sphere."

About a century and a half after the beginning of Gothic art in France there came an awakening or rebirth of art in Italy which we know as the period of the Renaissance. Starting in the ancient little town of Pisa, it soon spread over all Italy, and in time all over Europe, and although the period is supposed to be from 1300 to 1600, its influence in art and architecture has gone on and on, not only in the old world but in the new. It was the age of new learning and, through the invention of printing, it became widely disseminated so that education was not confined to the nobles alone, but spread to the masses. It was an age of science when Copernicus, the astronomer, discovered the revolution of the earth, and Galileo at Pisa, the law of the pendulum. It was an age of travel and discovery when Marco Polo made his journey to China and brought back tales of the fabulous riches of the East, and Columbus discovered a new world in the West. It was an age when Donatello, Michelangelo, Della Robbia, Brunelleschi, and a host of other great sculptors and architects were creating a new world of art; and architecture, after it had lain dormant for eight hundred years, once again flourished and culminated in the building of the great church of St. Peter's at Rome.

To me it has always seemed that these three hundred years marked the most interesting period in the world's history, particularly in art. The Renaissance was an awakening to a new life of marvelous beauty after the long period of rest following the decline of the Holy Roman Empire.

And so it has always been since the beginning of history — a period of progress, then a period of decline, over and over again. But the influence of this great movement was to go on and on and spread to every part of Europe and the western world.

Either consciously or unconsciously, the spirit of the Renaissance has an influence on us all, in some way. In the city where I live, a many-storied office building was erected some years ago which was an adaptation of the Flemish Gothic architecture. At the time it was built, everyone laughed at it with its high-pitched, gabled roof. Now we have learned to appreciate it and enjoy it because it is good art, after the type of the Guild halls and Cloth halls which came into being towards the end of the Renaissance period. Some of these exquisite buildings were destroyed by artillery during the German occupation of Belgium in the World War and of course can never be replaced.

We are apt to think of the disastrous aftereffects of this terrible war in terms of dollars and cents, and in a secondary way, perhaps, we think of the loss of the flower of young manhood of the generation that fought it. But how seldom we stop to realize that the war not only destroyed the lives of many young men who might have become the greatest artists, sculptors or architects of their generation, but it also destroyed a great deal of fine architecture exemplified in the beautiful buildings in continental Europe, and brought the development of the fine arts to a more complete standstill than the world has known in many ages.

The eighteenth and nineteenth centuries witnessed a tremendous development in what we might call modern art and architecture. This was especially true in France, and Paris became the great art center and the most beautiful capital of the world. Streets and boulevards, parks and plazas were created with a lavish hand. Fountains and monuments were erected everywhere. The Louvre became the great storehouse for painting and sculpture, and the city itself, planned to symmetric building, gave the effect of a glorious whole with the Arc de Triomphe as its crowning point.

But enough of the old world where these arts were born. Let us come to the Western Hemisphere and see what progress has been made on this side of the Atlantic.

Two years ago the writer made a trip to South America, visiting the large cities of Santiago, Buenos Aires, Montevideo, Rio de Janeiro and Sao Paulo. The thing that impressed me most about South America was the beauty of its larger cities. We have nothing to compare with them in North America unless it be Washington, D. C. Not only are they beautifully planned, but every boulevard, park, public playground or plaza is tastefully adorned with good sculpture. This is especially true in Buenos Aires where law requires a public park or breathing space every three or four blocks even in the center of the business districts, and invariably a fine piece of sculpture will adorn its center.

The question arises, why are they so far ahead of us in civic planning and the appreciation of beauty in their cities? The answer is, because they are Latins, and the Latins have always beautified their cities as perhaps no other race in all history, unless we except the Greeks. They do not put a Greek temple here and a Roman forum there; a Gothic church on the corner and a Tudor house across the street, and then sprinkle in a few modernistic skyscrapers anywhere. They are more consistent and uniform without being monotonous, and the general effect is more like the grandeur that is Paris.

And now at last we come to our own country. What of the art of the United States? Well, we got off to a bad start. To quote Lorado Taft again, "Our ancestors here in this land were without sculptural tradition. Generally of humble origin, they had the prejudices of their class and seem to have attributed all of the arts to the devil. One dallied with them at his peril! To the Pilgrim Fathers, the churchly decorations were especially anathema, for they represented popery and idolatry. Their brothers in England delighted in breaking the Cathedral statuary, in burning religious paintings." What wonder then, I say, that in coming to the bleak and inhospitable New England shores there was no incentive within or without to go in for art, and it was to be two whole centuries before any sculptors appeared. Strange to relate, when one finally did develop, it was a little Quaker lady named Patience Wright, of New Jersey, who carved images in wax. To be sure, before this the cavaliers of Virginia, who perhaps best represented the wealth and culture of the day had been importing some fine sculpture from France to adorn their homes. But in 1781 the state of Virginia, through the influence of that far-sighted patron of the arts, Thomas Jefferson, commissioned the great French sculptor, Houdon, to come to this country to make a life-sized statue of Washington. This wonderful piece of work stands in the rotunda of the Capitol at Richmond, and I never go to that city without making a point of seeing it and admiring its beauty.

There seem to be several reasons why this country was so late in its appreciation and development of art: first, the frowning upon it by our perhaps over-pious Puritan ancestors; next, the tremendous influx of many nationalities, most of whom were from the lower strata of European populations, without well developed aesthetic sense; and finally, our own devotion to the almighty dollar to the neglect of the cultural matters. We were building a new country, not beautifying it.

Thus it was only within the last century that American sculptors began to appear, and practically all the progress in the fine arts that has been made has come during the memory of many people now living. Perhaps no country has ever made such a rapid advance in so short a space of time. We have not only made up our lost time but have actually gone ahead of many of the countries of the old world in sculpture and painting.

The history of American sculpture is almost told in the statues of George Washington to be found in practically every part of the world. One that is probably seen by more people every day than any other is the one by J. Q. A. Ward, a noted early American sculptor. This statue stands on the steps of the sub-treasury building in New York and represents Washington taking the oath of office. I think my favorite of all is the one by Daniel Chester French of "Washington the Crusader," a copy of which is to be seen in South Chicago. The original was a gift from this country to Paris. Of course we in the West will have the largest stone likness of the "Father of His Country" when Gutzon Borglum finishes his gigantic head on a far off mountain side in South Dakota.

To give more than a bare outline of the great work done in sculpture in this country during the past fifty years is impossible here; all I will attempt is to mention a few of the things I myself have seen and enjoyed.

This branch af the Arts seems to have received its impulse during the great expositions. The Centennial at Philadelphia in 1876, for the first time, brought European art into competition with American art. The World's Fair in Chicago in 1893 was the most glorious exhibition of art and architecture ever held at any fair. Everyone who saw them will always remember the beautiful McMonnies Fountain, the unique architecture of the

Transportation Building, and a hundred other unforgettable works of that time. This fair stimulated interest in art in this country as no other thing had ever done. It made the masses art conscious for the first time. And so on through all the fairs held since, including the last one at Chicago when we saw for the first time modernistic architecture in all its practical severity.

Not long ago I spent a day drinking in the architectural beauties of Canterbury cathedral in old England. A week later I was in the offices of a firm of architects in New York, and they were showing me the preliminary plans for the great New York Fair to be held in 1939. To me it looked as though someone had been playing with a lot of children's blocks, making geometrical designs with a big ball as the central motif. That may be a modernist's idea of fine architectural design, but I think the creators of it must have believed with Goethe that "Art is long, life short; judgment difficult and opportunity transient."

Everyone seems to agree that Augustus Saint Gaudens was our greatest sculptor, but of all the wonderful things that he did, the one that I like best is his Deacon Chapin or "The Puritan" in the public square at Springfield, Massachusetts. Here the old deacon with his high hat and flowing robe, with his cane in one hand and Bible in the other, stalking along on his way to church, is the very essence of fine art. One should never go to New York without viewing Saint Gaudens' equestrian "Sherman," or to Washington without seeing "The Peace of God," or to Boston without a visit to the "Shaw Memorial," or to Chicago without seeing his great "Lincoln." There are, of course, many other very great ones, but I mention these because I know them.

Richard Watson Gilder wrote of Saint Gaudens' works:

> *"Once lo! these shapes were not, now do they live,*
> *And shall forever in the hearts of men;*
> *And from their life new life shall spring again,*
> *To souls unborn new light and joy to give,*
> *Victory, Victory, he hath won the fight!"*

My favorite American sculptor is the late Daniel Chester French. Perhaps this is because I spent one delightful afternoon with him in his studio in New York. He was working at the time on his bronze statue of Judge James Green, later to be placed on the campus of Kansas University, and it was the writer's privilege to be on the committee to employ him for this work. He was so kindly and so hospitable. He showed me, among other things, the small working model for his heroic "Lincoln" which, as we know, is now a national shrine in the Lincoln Memorial at Washington. Those of you who can remember that far back, will recall that at the Columbian Exposition his "Death Staying the Hand of the Young Sculptor" was an epic, and it still is. French was not only a great sculptor but a kindly gentleman, which seems to be characteristic of the profession.

Lorado Taft I knew personally from the time I was a small boy when he came to our house in Lawrence, Kansas, to model a bust of Governor Charles Robinson, for the University. Taft probably did more in an educational way for art in America than any other man. He taught in the Art Institute in Chicago for years, gave thousands of lectures over the country, and executed some of our best sculpture. His "Fountain of Time" I do not care for, but I never go to Chicago without spending at least a little time before his delightful "Great Lakes" fountain at the south side of the Art Institute.

Gutzon Borglum came to our town once, and I had the pleasure of entertaining him. He is the exact opposite of the Saint Gaudens or French type, but a very interesting fellow, and the great group of American historical characters which he is carving on a mountain side in South Dakota will outlast any work of art in this country, at least in a physical way, if in no other.

A very popular and entertaining book which came out recently was Malvina Hoffman's *Heads and Tales*. In this book the author, who is one of our most noted living sculptors, tells of her experiences and adventures during trips all over the world in search of types from which to model her statues for the "Hall of Man," now to be seen in its entirety at the Field Museum at Chicago. I spent a Sunday afternoon at the Museum not long ago and was amazed at the stream of people who were there to see this remarkable collection of the work of one woman. In this stupendous undertaking she has reproduced in life-sized figures practically every race on the face of the globe, and the work is excellent. It is well worth a trip to Chicago to see.

Of course there are a host of other great sculptors I have not mentioned. I am only attempting to speak of a few examples of work I know and especially like. Every city of any size now can boast of some good sculpture either in its museums or public parks. But do we go to see them? I am afraid not. If we go to London, Paris, Rome or to the German art centers, the first thing we do is to go to the Art Museums, but if we Americans visit a great American city, these are the last places we visit if, indeed, we go to them at all.

Not much time will be taken in the discussion of architecture in America. It is true that there are literally thousands of wonderfully beautiful buildings in this country, but from the time when Charles Bulfinch designed our great Capitol building at Washington, which after all, is copied from the Roman style, down almost to the present, nothing original was being done. To quote from *Sticks and Stones,* "We have not lacked architects of boldness and originality, from Latrobe to Louis H. Sullivan. Nor have we lacked men of great ability, from Thomas Jefferson to Bertram Goodhue, nor yet have we lacked men who stood outside the currents of their time and kept their own position from Richardson to Dr. Cram. With all these capacities at our disposal, our finest efforts in building remain chaotic and undisciplined and dispersed — the reflection of our accumulated civilization." We were mere copyists, and we are still going through a period of gestation, but a few decades ago we began new building for a new age, and the skyscraper was born — an age of steel and concrete, an age of the practical and the utilitarian. It is a truism that our architectural development is bound up with the course of our civilization, and also our style of building is governed largely by economic reasons. When land in the large cities became so valuable, buildings could not afford to spread out; they shot up, and for the first time in our short history, something original in architecture appeared in our country. I often wonder what will come out of our present-day modernistic building both for business and residence purposes. At first I could not tolerate it, but with the years it is becoming less startling and more sane, and I am gradually becoming reconciled. But I still know that if I had to live in a modernistic house, I would feel as though I were living in a glass showcase and a very severe and barren one at that.

The work of one more American architect I must mention — that of Frank Lloyd Wright. His work is so unique, so impractical, but after all so practical that it has become world famous. Some years ago I spent several days at the Imperial Hotel in Tokyo. I thought it a very ugly and impractical piece of architecture. It was built, you know, on an immense, floating concrete base, and everyone said at the time it would be a colossal failure, but it was the only large building to withstand the two great earthquakes in Tokyo, and today it stands a monument to that great man who said that it could be done.

No article, however brief, on "Art in Its Three Dimensions" should fail to mention the latest and perhaps the most rapid development of art, that of photography as expressed in the moving picture. During the last twenty or thirty years we have all seen this industry grow from infancy to one of the finest forms of fine art. One only has to witness the showing of a picture made a decade ago as compared to some of the beautiful things being produced today to realize what giant strides have been made towards perfection in this art in such a short time. First came those flat, commonplace things made with inferior film using crudely painted backgrounds, with no attempt at beauty — simply story-telling. Then came sound, and then color. And now I am told they are striving to produce the third dimension. When this comes, and I am sure it will in the near future, we will have approached perfection in a new form of art. Most of the credit for this must go to America, and it will be the first form of art in which this new country has excelled! As I have said, color has done much to take away the flatness of black and white photography. It gives contrast and therefore depth to pictures, aside from the greatly enhanced beauty of the scene, if the colors are skillfully handled. We have gone a long way, but the third dimension has yet to be accomplished. One of our great grand opera singers, Tito Schipa, was recently quoted as saying, "The great operas can never be adequately produced in motion pictures until accurate perspective or optical depth is perfected for the scene." Only the other day I had a letter from a New York amateur photographer in which he said, "Have you seen or heard of three dimension photography? Recently I had the almost unbelievable experience of seeing a photographic film of a dish of fruit so realistic as to make me want to reach for an apple that was in the dish." With the tremendous amount of money and talent now being devoted to the development of the third dimension in photography, it will undoubtedly be only a short time until this great dream becomes a reality.

An unpublished, satiric drawing of the eighties shows a family of American tourists in the Louvre. They contemplate the Melian Venus. With one exception they are dumb with awe. The exception is Aunt Maria, the masterful old lady in the foreground. Aunt Maria has seen men and cities, but she doesn't know as there's much that can beat South Bend. So —

> *Aunt Maria gazes with distrust*
> *Upon the goddess in her bloom perennial,*
> *'Talk about art — you should have seen the bust,*
> *The butter bust we had at our Centennial.'*

THE PAGEANT OF KANSAS HISTORY. FRED M. TORREY, SCULPTOR

This seems to represent the status of the average local mind in its appreciation of sculpture, at least until only a few years ago. The cow carved in butter at the State Fair was the only piece of sculpture in town, and it was on exhibition for but one week in the year.

Some years ago a far-sighted governor of the state of Nebraska appointed a citizens' committee of highly intelligent men to build a new state Capitol at Lincoln. My old friend, William E. Hardy, a business man who had travelled extensively and had seen good architecture all over the world, headed the commission. They employed Bertram Grosvenor Goodhue, one of the greatest architects this country has produced, and years were spent in planning and building the structure. The result of this honest and intelligent work is the finest state capitol building in the United States, indeed one of the best examples of architecture in the entire country.

It was my good fortune to be on the building committee of a board of education at a time when the city had voted more than two million dollars for the construction of a new high school. Here was a real opportunity to do something outstanding in a public building. It was at a time when the school board was a highly intelligent body, and the public co-operative in every way. We were extremely fortunate in securing almost four blocks of beautifully landscaped ground in the heart of the city for a site. The board, especially the building committee, spent almost a year visiting the best and newest high schools all over the country before a single plan was drawn. Two years later the building was completed. There was much hard work as well as much real pleasure, a great deal of criticism, but in the end almost universal praise. It has been said by many good judges of fine architecture from various parts of the United States, to be the most beautiful and practical high school building in the country.

Two years ago, a prominent Topeka, Kansas, woman, at her death, left by her will, fifty thousand dollars for the erection of a monument commemorating the native sons and daughters of Kansas. The sum left for this noble purpose is probably the largest ever given for a single work of art in this part of the country. There was considerable criticism at the time, many persons thinking it should have been left to some charitable undertaking. But the donor had already given twice that sum during her lifetime to build a hospital wing, and her wish was to do something for her city that would, if properly done, be "a thing of beauty and a joy forever." The five trustees selected by the donor, of which I happened to be one, recognized the responsibility placed upon them in undertaking this service, and after looking the field over very carefully selected Fred M. Torrey, a sculptor of Chicago and a favorite pupil of the late Lorado Taft, to design and execute the work. The design chosen comprises a long panel or frieze of Bedford limestone with an over-all length of eighty feet upon the face of which is to be carved an historical pageant of figures in bold relief. These figures tell the story of Kansas history from the time of the Indian down to the present, with the covered wagon of pioneer days as the central motif. On a pedestal in front of this great panel are to be two figures in bronze of heroic size representing the native son and native daughter dressed in the costumes of pioneer days. In front of all a sunken garden is to be placed, and with tall trees for a background and proper landscaping in the foreground, the group as a whole will be one of the most beautiful and imposing things of its kind in America.

What of the architecture in the average American city today? My answer to this question is that, as a whole, it is very bad and not improving very rapidly. The reason for this is that Topsy-like, we have just "growed up" with the country, a country that has been too busy with other things to pay much attention to civic beauty. We have made little effort in selecting any particular type of building to suit its locality, and a start toward city planning has come only in the last few years. City planning boards are usually composed of men who are political appointees and have little or no knowledge of what it is all about, and are therefore mere figureheads. Fortunately, this is not true in some of our larger cities, such as Cleveland and Chicago where great strides have been made in civic improvement in the last few years.

Recently I visited a typical midwestern city and started out to see the town. Leaving the business center, I passed through the inevitable slum district with its ramshackle, unpainted frame buildings — a depressing start. Next came some of the one-time "swell" houses, the Mansard roof variety, a horrible style of architecture, a relic of the roaring eighties, and most likely used now for cleaning and dyeing establishments or perhaps "beauty parlors!" Next came the pressed brick mansion of the gay nineties, today perhaps degenerated into second-class boarding houses; then blocks of two-story, nondescript frame houses so popular at the turn of the century. The bungalow belt came next, not so unsightly, but certainly not adapted to the climate of the locality. Finally on the outskirts of town, I arrived at the fine, new residential district. Here were some beautiful homes, but what a conglomeration of types of architecture! There were English, Colonial, Mission, Spanish, a German Gothic next to a French chateau, fairly glaring at each other, and finally, a pile of square blocks with huge windows, known as modernistic. Period architecture run riot!

I retraced my steps to the downtown public building district, with, perhaps, an over-critical eye and in a depressed mood. The courthouse was just — courthouse. No one, by any possible chance could mistake it for anything else, because there are ten thousand others in the country, just like it. Out on the street stood a huge statue of "Justice." I think some sculptor once had these "Justices" made up by the hundred. One sees them everywhere. The city library was located next to the railroad station, where the whistling and clanging of trains made one smile at the motto over the door, "Speech is silver, silence is golden."

The large city auditorium was situated amid depressing surroundings with no chance for landscaping and very little parking space; evidently located there for purely political reasons. The schools all seemed to be labeled, "Why hire an architect? We already had a set of plans." No individuality, no attempt at originality or beauty, no thought of fitness to the locality; simply the old, square, buff brick type that school boards have been turning out by the thousands for the past half century.

Of course there are a few bright spots in every city, and many of them in the larger ones. But this is a picture of one town that I saw, and it is a fairly representative example of the average American city.

Now the reason for all this is that the choice of location and type of architecture for most of our public buildings is left to city and county commissioners and school boards whose members are in office for only a few short years at best (or worst), and who as a rule have had little education along these lines, no experience in building, and most certainly small appreciation for good art and architecture. This condition will continue until some day, the American people will wake up and insist upon having planning and building boards made up of men and women who have wide experience, a high degree of intelligence and a real and lasting interest in the beautification of their city.

This is a bewildering period in American history. We are a polyglot nation made up of people who have poured into this country from all over the world. We started out without any original ideas in art. We were mere copyists of what other countries had done. Today we have more "isms" than all the other countries put together. We are a national crucible of heterogeneous matter as far as art is concerned. But we have developed and are developing great artists, sculptors and architects, and out of this crucible must come an ultimate refinement of art such as this country has never known. The story of American sculpture and architecture is but just begun.

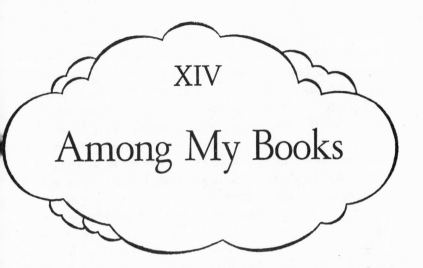

XIV

Among My Books

ALL MY LIFE I have been a collector of something. I started out as a small boy collecting tobacco tags and cigarette pictures, then postage stamps, then autographs and later, much later, books! I think that if I should be cast away on a desert island, I would begin collecting sea shells. It is a virus, once in the blood, never are you able to get rid of it.

Some years ago I built a house. The library was the big end of it and the rest merely incidental. The room is a rather large one, twenty-four by forty feet, and two stories high. Around the four walls are shelves, which hold about six thousand volumes, the accumulation of a lifetime. A balcony gives access to books above.

Often I have thought that I detected on the faces of friends who have visited me in this room an expression that I have thus interpreted: "Where did this man get all these books? Did he inherit them or buy them by the yard or by the piece? Does he read them or are they merely a beautiful background to the room — friends he never cuts? It is true there is an old Latin maxim, 'Beware the man of one book,' but isn't he overdoing it to catch his visitor unawares?"

The answer to that unasked question, I now take up as a labor of love — and hence this intimate, personal record of how my library came into being, of how it grew through the years and of the associations it has brought with other books and bookmen. So I ask the reader to imagine himself one of those inquiring friends, comfortably seated in an easy chair in my library.

A glance around the balcony, with its row on row of uniform bindings, might suggest to you that these books, at least, were bought by the yard. But there you would be greatly mistaken, for they are bound volumes of magazines, acquired month by month, volume by volume over a period of nearly ninety years, by two generations.

My father, a born booklover, was an original subscriber to *Harper's Magazine* when it was started in 1850, and five years later when the *Atlantic Monthly* put in an appearance, and he arrived in Kansas, he bought the first number and kept it up until his death in 1900. When Quantrill and his men burned and sacked Lawrence in 1863, about all that father saved out of this terrible massacre was his life and some of his books and magazines. Of course, they have become very dear to me, not on account of their intrinsic worth, which is considerable, but for their history and sentimental value, and I have kept them, read them and added to them, month by month, for the past forty years. There are perhaps no other two magazines published over a long period of years that would better tell the history of writing, printing and illustrating in this country.

Along with the magazines on the balcony are seven large volumes of the *New York Semi-weekly Tribune* covering the Civil War years, Horace Greeley's time. Here is the day by day newspaper story of history in the making, and it is extremely interesting to pore over these great volumes as I have been doing, lo, these many years. What a thrill there is in reading Lincoln's Emancipation Proclamation as it was printed the very hour of its release to the press, or the account of the Battle of Gettysburg, day by

150

day, or in speculating with the editor whether or not Grant will finally take Vicksburg, or in watching in each issue the daily progress of the Army of the Tennessee. That even war had its bright side, may be traced in the financial reports that U. S. Government 6's may be purchased at ninety-six and a half, or that the farmer is receiving twenty dollars a ton for his hay. Those, indeed, were the good old days.

But to answer another question, does the owner read all of these books? The answer is No! Decidedly not. He reads some of them, has, in fact, over many years read a great many of them, but in a library of this character and size, one is not expected to read every volume. Can anyone say that he has read the *Encyclopedia Britannica* for instance?

As Eugene Field wrote in his *Love Affairs of a Bibliomaniac*, "There are very many kinds of book collectors, but I think all may be grouped in three classes, viz.; those who collect from vanity; those who collect for the benefit of learning; those who collect through a veneration and love for books."

Personally, I plead guilty on all three counts and will add a fourth, those who collect rare books and manuscripts for their rarity and beauty, and for the pleasure and instruction they may give not only to the owner but other kindred souls to whom they may be shown. One may own a rare first edition, an early Latin Bible, a Shakespeare in the first folio or a poem in original manuscript, and love them, each one, for their rarity and beauty. But to read them or lend them out to be read,— No, they are too precious for that; they deserve a higher respect from the man fortunate enough to own them. This reminds me of Austin Dobson's poem:

MY BOOKS

"They dwell in the odor of camphor,
They stand in a Sheraton Shrine ,
They are warranted early editions,
These worshipped tomes of mine.

In their creamy 'Oxford Vellum',
In their redolent 'Crushed Levant',
With their delicate watered linings,
They are jewels of price, I grant: —

Blind-tooled and Morocco jointed,
They have Bedford's daintiest dress,
They are graceful, attentuate, polished,
But they gather the dust, no less: —

For the row that I prize is yonder,
Away on the unglazed shelves,
The bulged and the bruised octavos,
The dear and the dumpy twelves,—

Montayne with his sheepskin blistered
And Howell the worse for wear,
And the Worm-drilled Jesuits' Horace,
And the little old cropped Molière,

And the Burton I bought for a florin,
And the Rabelais foxed and flea'd, —
For the others I never have opened,
But those are the ones I read."

It is said that it takes a lot of living in a house to make it a home — so it might be said also, a collection of books does not become a library unless it has been acquired book by book with loving care and no little knowledge and appreciation, over the years.

But let us go back to the very beginning. I well remember the day I acquired my first books, *The Lovers of the World,* in three volumes, given as a bonus with a year's subscription to *Collier's.* A humble beginning, but the books still occupy an honored place in my library. The next books I bought came hard. I was working seventeen hours a day in a drug store for sixty dollars a month, but managed to save enough out of this sum to pay my installments on a set of Thackeray which I read in the evenings when business was slack. One set led to another until I had a reasonably good though small collection of the great American poets and of English masters of the novel.

Poor RICHARD improved:

BEING AN
ALMANACK
AND
EPHEMERIS
OF THE
MOTIONS of the SUN and MOON;
THE TRUE
PLACES and ASPECTS of the PLANETS;
THE
RISING and *SETTING* of the *SUN;*
AND THE
Rising, Setting *and* Southing *of the* Moon,
FOR THE
YEAR of our LORD 1763:
Being the Third after LEAP-YEAR.

Containing also,

The Lunations, Conjunctions, Eclipses, Judgment of the Weather, Rising and Setting of the Planets, Length of Days and Nights, Fairs, Courts, Roads, &c. Together with useful Tables, chronological Observations, and entertaining Remarks.

Fitted to the Latitude of Forty Degrees, and a Meridian of near five Hours West from *London*; but may, without sensible Error, serve all the NORTHERN COLONIES.

By *RICHARD SAUNDERS*, Philom.

PHILADELPHIA:
Printed and Sold by B. FRANKLIN, and D. HALL.

TITLE PAGE OF ONE OF BENJAMIN FRANKLIN'S
POOR RICHARD ALMANACKS

Then came Dumas, Daudet, Gautier, Hugo, Merimée and Eugene Sue, a regular orgy of the French novelists, read, alas, in English. My scholarly friends tell me that novels written in foreign languages are so much better before translation. Russian literature came next, when I bought a set of Turgenev, and for a year I revelled in it. Next came German, Norwegian and Swedish books. In fact I was going along very well, acquiring standard works from good presses, in good commercial bindings, perhaps foot by foot, when something happened that opened up a new world to me, one of whose existence I had been hitherto blissfully unconscious.

It was the rare book world, and I drifted into it so easily and innocently that before I realized it the virus of this hobby had entered my system. Once this disease gets a firm hold on you, you may as well give up, you will never get over it.

My mother had been on a trip East to her old home in Pennsylvania, and in delving into a barrel in the old home attic, she had come upon a lot of dust covered, dog-eared almanacs. Bundling them up, she brought them home to me "on suspicion." An examination of the queer looking pamphlets revealed the fact that they were twenty-five years of original *Poor Richard's Almanacks,* which were published by Benjamin Franklin in Philadelphia during the last half of the eighteenth century and are now among the rarest of Americana.

Some months later I took them to New York to be bound, and was delighted to learn that I was the possessor of the third largest collection of these famous almanacs in existence at that time, the largest collection being in the Historical Society of Pennsylvania. I have acquired ten or twelve more years of the almanacs since then, but there are now, no doubt, several other collections which exceed mine.

Shortly after I had begun to cultivate a taste for first editions, I learned that a small library of a deceased, distant relative was to be sold at auction in Lawrence, Kansas, and that it contained a copy of the first edition of *Uncle Tom's Cabin,* in two volumes, published in Boston in 1852, in the original binding, each volume bearing a presentation inscription to one of my cousins, by Mr. and Mrs. Stowe. On the day of the auction, bidding for the books was spirited. Starting at a dollar and a half, the bids quickly ran up to six dollars and a quarter, at which price competition ceased and the prize was mine. Today these books, with their inscriptions are unique, and if I were to tell you what they would bring, you probably would not believe me. I have no compunctions as to the price I paid as there were only distant heirs, and I think the former owner would be glad to know the volumes fell into appreciative hands.

My rambles, at home and abroad, among the rare book dealers, collectors, printers and writers have brought acquaintances in many cities. Among them are the Drake boys in New York City, who have succeeded their good father, James F. Drake, dealer in American "Firsts"; Walter Hill and George M. Chandler in Chicago; Charles Goodspeed in Boston; Doctor A. S. W. Rosenbach in Philadelphia; John Howell, father and son, in San Francisco; and the Dawsons, father and son again, in Los Angeles; and a host of others in this country. Then abroad I have book-dealer friends in London, Paris, Berlin and Vienna. All book dealers seem to be endowed with wonderful memories; like the elephant, they never forget. Once I walked into Maggs' Brothers in London after an absence of many years. Much to my surprise, Mr. Maggs greeted me with, "How do you do, Mr. Woodward. Where have you been keeping yourself all these years?" Their memory for books bought and sold is even more remarkable.

At Dawson's Book Shop in Los Angeles, one is always running into interesting people, not the least of whom is Dorothy Bevis, an authority on Incunabula, author of a book of poems, *Silver Farthing,* and as I have often told her, she is the best book salesman on two continents. One time I saw in this shop a man who looked familiar to me. "Isn't that Hugh Walpole?" I asked.

"It certainly is," Miss Bevis replied. "Stick around and I will give you an introduction." The introduction soon followed, and we had a long talk on books and pictures. Walpole was at the time writing the "David Copperfield" scenario for the movies.

At another time I met there Robert E. Cowan, the great authority on Californiana. He was then librarian of the very wonderful William Andrews Clark Library in Los Angeles, and he invited me out to visit it. Of course, I accepted. It was an opportunity to see one of the great private libraries in America in a very intimate way. That afternoon I arrived at the Clark estate and found the library a beautiful white marble building set in an Italian garden.

Inside, I was conducted to a great room finished in true medieval style. Seating myself on an old oak bench, I said, "Mr. Cowan, there are three excessively rare books in this library that I should particularly like to hold in my own hands. They are the first edition of Gray's *Elegy,* the copy of Poe's *Tamerlane* and Mr. Clark's fine copy of the *First Folio of Shakespeare.*"

"No sooner said than done," he replied, and presently he returned from the stack room and laid the three precious volumes before me and then left me with them. There I sat for the next two hours, alone in that great hall, with no one to disturb me, reverently turning the leaves of volumes worth a king's ransom. It was indeed a bibliophile's paradise.

One more good friend is Douglas C. McMurtrie of Chicago. Mr. McMurtrie, author of many books about books, is probably best known for his *The Golden Book,* recently superseded by a larger and better volume entitled *The Book: The Story of Printing and Bookmaking.* This man has done much for the betterment of typography in America.

It has never been my good fortune to meet A. Edward Newton, but we have corresponded, and I have a whole shelf of his autographed editions which, I think, I read and reread more than any other books I own.

156

Following in the wake of such acquaintanceships, or perhaps, more truly, when one's name is once listed in the Red Book of rare book collectors, comes a daily arrival of catalogues from all parts of the world. Some of these are truly works of art, beautifully printed and illustrated; others merely mimeographed sheets, but they are always storehouses of interest and information for the collector, and one must read them if one is to keep posted on current prices.

One day, a few years ago, I was on the point of throwing a catalogue of the cheapest class, from a dealer in Albany, into the fire when my eye caught the following item: *"The Agriculturists' Almanack* for nine years, with the diary of Dr. William Darlington, the scientist, interleaved." As the doctor happened to have been my mother's uncle, I wired at once for the books and in due time received them. The diary written in the early nineteenth century proved to be a veritable history of the time, as Dr. Darlington saw it and played a part in it, and sometime I hope to publish it. Shortly after receiving these almanacs I had a letter from the United States Department of Agriculture asking if they might purchase them from me for their library. I refused to sell, telling them it was a personal diary of an ancestor. They replied in an appreciative way saying they did not blame me for wishing to keep them, under the circumstances.

Some years ago my father's library of about fifteen hundred volumes came to me, and these books were merged with my own. His library consisted largely of poetry, essays, art and biography, and did much to round out the weak spots in my own collection.

Along with the taste for rare books came a desire to collect all phases of this mania: first editions, extra illustrated books, examples of the great binders, incunabula, manuscripts, English color-plate books, association books, limited editions from modern private presses, books in original parts, fore-edge painting, rare translations and others, and the library now contains examples of these various branches of bibliography.

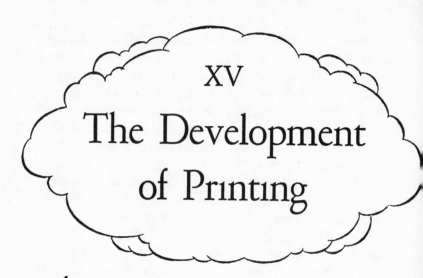

XV

The Development of Printing

A FEW YEARS ago I became intensely interested in the history of printing from the earliest times down to the present. It occurred to me that it would be a great satisfaction to own a sequence of examples of this great art, and I now possess a more or less complete collection covering a period of over four thousand years. From this collection, selections have been made for exhibition purposes at various colleges and universities, and they have never failed to excite interest among students of the art of printing.

Starting with a Babylonian clay tablet of about 2250 B. C., my next example is a Coptic manuscript on papyrus, written about 600 A. D. Following this comes an Italian illuminated manuscript of the fourteenth century, and then a French illuminated missal or mass-book on vellum dated 1450, produced just about the time of the invention of printing by Gutenberg.

A leaf from the Gutenberg Bible, the first important book to be printed from movable types, is one of the treasures of the collection. There are perhaps a dozen examples of incunabula or books printed during the years 1450 to 1500, known as the Golden Age of printing. Chief among these is a *Nuremberg Chronicle,* one of the well-known early illustrated printed books, a copy of Sebastian Brant's *Stultifera Navis,* or *Ship of Fools,* a Livy, a Horace, a St. Thomas Aquinas, printed in 1480, and a delightfully illuminated manuscript, *Hours of the Virgin,* from the library of William Morris. Another interesting item is a fifteenth century English Horn book of which only a few remain in existence.

Speaking of Horn books perhaps calls for some information as to what they are and how they came to be made and used. Back in the days when books were scarce and very expensive, children learned their ABC's from a Horn book. It consisted of a piece of leather or wood shaped like a hand mirror, with the alphabet printed in large letters on paper attached to the top side and covered with a piece of horn to preserve it. A string was tied to the handle, and the book hung around the child's neck; not only handy but a great protection against childish destructiveness. Horn books were used even in this country during colonial times.

In addition to these, there are in the library about three hundred one-page examples of practically all the great presses of Germany, Italy, France, Spain, the Netherlands and England during the fifteenth century, and fifty examples of woodcut prints made during that period. There are two nice Caxton leaves (I could never afford a complete book), a little Latin grammar from the press of Wynken de Worde, Caxton's successor, and a Richard Pynson, representing the three great English printers of the fifteenth century, and several from the press of the Venetian pioneer in making books truly comfortable to read, Aldus Manutius.

Coming down the line into the sixteenth century there are several good examples of the Aldine classics, printed by Aldus, the Younger, including a Cicero, a little book from the Gryphus Press, 1545, and a small example from the celebrated press of Christopher Plantin.

FIFTEENTH CENTURY LEATHER HORN BOOK

I will mention only two books that I have, printed in the seventeenth century, a graceful Caesar from the famous Elzevier Press dated 1635, and the first collected edition of Francis Bacon printed in London in 1638.

The eighteenth century printing is best exemplified by the press of Benjamin Franklin, not only in the Almanacs already mentioned, but by several other items, including a copy of Cicero's *Cato Major,* probably the best piece of printing Franklin ever did and one of the rarest of Americana.

The nineteenth century witnessed a Renaissance of the art of printing, especially in England. In the library are some good examples of that period including Chaucer's *Canterbury Tales* from the famous Kelmscott Press of William Morris, perhaps the finest piece of printing of modern times, books from the Doves Press of Cobden-Sanderson, the scholarly editions of Keats and Shelley by Buxton-Foreman, the Murray edition of Goldsmith, the lovely Wreath edition of Edmund Spenser and others too numerous to mention.

The twentieth century, with its many fine private presses is, of course, well represented, the latest acquisition being made recently in London, a volume from the well-known Ashendene Press, Chelsea.

In first editions there is first and foremost in importance a complete Shakespeare play, *A Midsummer-Night's Dream,* from the first folio, 1623. Next I might mention Dr. Johnson's famous *Dictionary* in two large volumes in their original bindings published in 1775; thirdly, Hawthorne's *Scarlet Letter,* 1850, thought by some to be the greatest American novel. This book has had a tremendous increase in price since I obtained my copy and is probably the best investment I ever made. There are many other good "Firsts," including the more important Thackeray novels, the Dickens *Christmas Books,* and *Edwin Drood* in original parts.

Books that have come from the libraries of famous personages are always interesting. Here we find, to mention a few, a seventeenth century book on the *Art of Preaching* from the library of Alexander Pope with his signature on a fly leaf; a religious work bound for Queen Anne with her royal crown stamped on the cover; a work on French artillery practice from Napoleon's library at Fontainebleau; a novel from Robert Louis Stevenson's library at Vailima; Thackeray's own copy of Keats' poems, with his library stamp on a fly leaf; Millard Fillmore's copy of the first edition of *Blackstone* with his name inscribed many times.

Of association books, or books inscribed by the author, the one I love the best is a first edition of *Over The Teacups* inscribed to my father by none other than Oliver Wendell Holmes himself. A little book, the first American edition of Oscar Wilde's poems is unique. Opposite the title page the author quotes, over his characteristic signature, from his beautiful poem, *The Garden of Eros,* "Creamy meadows sweet, whiter than Juno's throat and odorous as all Arabia." And on another blank page opposite the poem, *Impression du Matin, a Thames Nocturne,* he writes: "Written one night walking home by the Thames with Whistler. He painted the scene and made a poem in color. I answered him by a picture in poetry." This must have occurred while the two men were such good friends and before Whistler wrote, *The Gentle Art of Making Enemies,* and practised it on his old friend, Oscar. Somehow the possession of this book always gives me the feeling of a personal acquaintance with the two men.

Once Edwin Markham visited me for several days, and before he left he inscribed in one of his volumes of poems, that famous quatrain: *Outwitted,*

> *"He drew a circle that shut me out —*
> *Heretic, rebel, a thing to flout.*
> *But love and I had the wit to win.*
> *We drew a circle that took him in!"*

Another modern writer's book that I prize is by my friend and fellow townsman, Doctor Karl A. Menninger. In his popular work, *The Human Mind,* he has written, "To my friend, who has taught me many things about books, and inspired an even greater love for them in me by his example."

One more is Max Miller's *Mexico Around Me,* in which he says, "Just to put away in that grand big library of yours." This book also has an extra illustration in color on a fly leaf done by the illustrator, Everett Gee Jackson. There is a whole shelf of others, and I love them all, knowing that the author himself has handled each particular volume.

There are many other association books, including Whittier, Longfellow, Theodore Roosevelt, John Burroughs and last but by no means least, copies of our own Dr. Charles M. Sheldon's book, *In His Steps,* more copies of which have been sold throughout the world than any other book, the Bible excepted.

Books bound by famous binders are next. Of course the old blind-tooled pigskin volumes of the fifteenth century are here in numbers, one with its iron chain still attached which locked it to its monastery shelf in the days of its youth, and it is remarkable how well preserved these are after five centuries of time and use. I have a book bound by Roger Paine, considered by many the greatest English binder of his time, and two by Samuel Mearne, who preceded him. There are examples of the comparatively modern English and French binders, including one by the great Frenchman Duru, and a filigree silver binding executed by a German binder.

The book that I love the best of all in my library is my copy of *Old Wine in New Bottles,* being a volume of poems and essays written by my father. The copy he inscribed to me I had Stikeman, who at the time was one of the best American binders, do for me according to a design of my own.

Of the extra illustrated books, I shall mention only one, Scott's own favorite edition of the Waverley novels, with not only the exquisite Turner plates but also those of Cruikshank and several others as well, beautifully bound by Root and Son of London.

CHARLES DICKENS' INK POT

To enumerate the English color plate books or the books from modern presses would make this article seem too much like a catalogue, so I shall not attempt it.

If one is a collector of rare books, manuscripts or autograph letters, opportunities come occasionally to acquire other items intimately connected with the lives of authors. I have in my possession a quaint old ink pot with the initials C. D. engraved upon it. Along with it is a letter written by Georgina Hogarth, Charles Dickens' sister-in-law and administrator of his estate, in which she testifies that her brother-in-law used this ink well both at Gad's Hill and Tavistock House over a period of years. When I hold this little object in my hand, I think of how many thousands of times Dickens must have dipped his pen in it, — maybe the ink that formed the words, "God bless us every one," came out of this very pot! What could be more intimately connected with him?

Lastly, let me assure you that I am not a student nor a scholar, merely a browser. I have always enjoyed being in the company of books, and although I say I do not buy books any more, yet somehow or other they keep accumulating.

If I had, in the beginning, concentrated on some one particular line of rare book collecting such as Frankliniana, Shakespeareana, Incunabula, first editions of some one author, or any one of a score of other branches of rare book collecting, I might with the opportunities I have had, be the possessor of a real library of note on a small scale. But the day has passed when a man of small means (comparatively speaking) can do such things. It is now a rich man's game. Some of the books I now own, acquired years ago, I could not begin to afford at present prices.

A few years ago A. Edward Newton began writing that delightful series of articles about rare books in the *Atlantic Monthly*. Dr. A. S. W. Rosenbach did the same thing in the *Saturday Evening Post*. These articles and others created a widespread interest in the game; many new recruits entered it, which caused a tremendous increase in prices. The law of supply and demand in regard to rare books is still in force, and although the demand has increased many fold, the supply constantly diminishes and prices go skyward.

A comparatively short time ago a copy of the Gutenberg Bible, best known of all rare books, sold for only a few thousand dollars. Much more recently, the Melk copy was presented to the Yale Library by Mrs. Harkness, she having paid the then top price of one hundred and twenty thousand dollars for it. In 1928 my friend, Dr. Otto H. F. Vollbehr of Berlin purchased the St. Paul copy on vellum for three hundred and five thousand dollars, the highest price ever paid for a book. Yet Dr. Rosenbach, the well known antiquary of Philadelphia, has predicted that the next price of a mere paper copy of this rare book will be more than a million dollars. This may well be, for there are only forty-five known copies of this most precious masterpiece in the whole world. Most of them have found permanent abiding places in the great libraries, and it may be many years before a copy comes on the market at any price.

About 1930, the United States Congress, without a dissenting voice, voted one and a half million dollars to acquire for the Library of Congress, the Vollbehr copy of the Bible, along with three thousand other titles of Incunabula, and as the years go by, the people of this country will realize more and more that, probably unwittingly, the seventy-first Congress thus performed one of the greatest acts of its career. The purchase of these monuments of the fifteenth century was not only a great bargain, but it was for this country one of the greatest single cultural steps in its history. So when we grow pessimistic about the achievements of our statesmen in Washington, let us not forget that by a single act and by unanimous vote of both houses this great cultural advancement was accomplished. This same Congress appropriated another seven million dollars to build additions planned to correct the overcrowded condition of our National Library.

William Dana Orcutt, noted authority on books, said "These two acts alone will transform the Library of Congress from a second or third rate depository of books into one of the greatest libraries of the world."

I recently asked my friend, Theodore Wesley Koch, noted translator of the classics and Librarian of Northwestern University, for his estimation of books in the home library, and he replied with the following:

THANKS TO BOOKS

"There they are, waiting and silent. They neither urge, nor call, nor press their claims. Mutely they are ranged along the wall. They seem to be asleep, yet from each one a name looks at you like on open eye. If you look their way or reach a hand toward them they do not call out, nor are they insistent. They make no demands. They wait until advances are made to them; then for the first time they open up. First, when there is quiet about us, peace within us; then we are ready for them. Some evening on returning from a tiresome round of duties, some day when one is weary of his fellow men, or in the morning when clouded and heavy with dream-laden sleep — only then is one ready for books. You would like to hold a parley and yet be alone. You would like to dream, but in music. With the pleasurable presentiment of a pleasant experiment you go to the bookcase: a hundred eyes, a hundred names silently and patiently meet your searching glance as the slave women of a seraglio look to their master, humbly awaiting the call, and yet blissful to be chosen. And then as the finger gropes about on the piano to find the key for a hidden melody, gently it yields to the hand, this dumb white thing, this closed violin — in it all the voices of God are locked up. You open up a book, you read a line, a verse; but it does not ring clear at the moment. Disappointed, you put it back almost roughly, until you find the right book for the moment. Then suddenly you are seized, you breathe rapidly and as you carry

167

it away to the lamp, The Book, the happily chosen volume glows, dazzles with an inner light. Magic has been done; from delicate clouds of dreams there stalks forth phantasmagoria. Broad vistas open up and your vanishing senses are lost in space.

"Little fragments of eternity, quietly ranged along the plain wall, you stand there unpretentiously in our home. Yet when the hand frees you, when the heart touches you, you break through the everyday prosy surroundings; your words lead us as in a fiery chariot up from pettiness into the eternal."

XVI

Shakespeare in America

$\mathcal{D}$ID WILLIAM SHAKESPEARE ever come to America? Of course, we know that he did not.

That is an even more absurd idea than that Bacon wrote his plays. But I read the other day that Shakespeare died worth about three hundred thousand dollars, which might indicate that he did come to this country and cleaned up on the stock market, because he certainly never could have made that much money out of play acting in England in his day. It is estimated that he did make something like six hundred pounds a year, some years, and that was big money in those times when the dollar went as far as ten will go today. Even if he were a rich man when he died, in his will, the sole bequest to his wife, Anne Hathaway, was the "second best bed and the furniture."

No, Will Shakespeare never came to America, but the products of his brain have been coming here, especially during the last quarter century, until there are more Shakespeareana in America today than there are in the country where he lived and worked.

But I am getting ahead of my story.

169

In 1923 there occurred the tercentenary celebration of the birth of the greatest book in all English literature, the publishing of the first folio of Shakespeare's plays in 1623, and this celebration seemed to awaken a keen interest among collectors of the early printing of Shakespeare's works, particularly for the first folio.

In the first place let me state what "folio" means in printing. The word comes from the Latin, *folium,* meaning a leaf, and in the early days of printing the unit of size was reckoned from the *folium,* which was a sheet of paper approximately nine by fourteen inches. From folding print paper in different sizes we get the quarto, the octavo and even smaller sizes. The first printing of Shakespeare's works was on folio size, hence we get the term, "first folio," distinguishing it from the second, third and fourth folios and the quartos which were printed a little later. The largest known copy of the first folio measures eight and three quarters by thirteen and a half inches.

It is, perhaps not commonly known that the first printing of Shakespeare's plays was not until seven years after his death. Shakespeare died in 1616 and the first folio, as has been said, was printed in 1623. The manuscripts of the plays, which appeared in the first folio, were gathered together by two men, Heming and Condell, friends and fellow actors of Shakespeare's company, who produced the book as a labor of love and in this way preserved, for all time, these great plays which would otherwise have been lost forever. The book was printed by Isaac Jaggard and Ed Blount and contained thirty-six plays. Heming and Condell have somewhere stated, "we have scarce received a blot in his papers" by which, doubtless, they implied that they had a fair copy from which to print.

We realize what a great debt of gratitude the world owes to these two men, Heming and Condell, when we stop to think that had it not been for the enterprise of literary pirates, who in some way, came into possession of these priceless manuscripts and the devotion of these friends after his death, Shakespeare might be little more than a name to us now.

It is acknowledged by all students of Shakespeareana that the first folio is far better than any of the succeeding folios both typographically and in correctness of text.

Not long after the printing of the first folio, all the manuscripts were destroyed either by the great fire of London, or by the Puritans, or both. Just how many copies of the first folio were printed, we do not know, but today there are only one hundred and fifty-six known copies in existence and these are in various conditions of cleanliness and completeness. Fourteen copies are in their original state of perfection. A perfect copy of the first folio must contain the well known picture of Shakespeare by Droeshout, used as a frontispiece, and a leaf of verses on the opposite page by his famous contemporary, Ben Jonson. A great many of the known copies lack this famous portrait and the opposite page.

Shakespeare, himself, published nothing during his lifetime, except two narrative poems, written during his early literary career, which are of but mediocre quality.

The first folio was not particularly noteworthy from the standpoint of the printer's art, although the printing and the paper have withstood the ravages of time better than much of the printing done in later years. It is the sentimental side of this work that makes it a wonderful thing, when we consider the fact that this is the only connecting link that saved the works of Shakespeare from utter destruction and extinction. With this now famous and memorable volume of his collected plays, known as the first folio, in mind, any of his contemporaries might well have told us that "He was not of an age, but for all time."

In 1756 a copy of the first folio sold for three guineas or about sixteen or seventeen dollars. This is the earliest record we have of a sale. In 1864 the George Daniels copy sold for seven hundred and sixteen pounds and was bought for the famous Baroness Bur-

171

A
MIDSOMMER
Nights Dreame.

Actus primus.

Enter Theseus, Hippolita, with others.

Theseus.

Ow faire Hippolita, our nuptiall houre
Drawes on apace: foure happy daies bring in
Another Moon: but oh, me thinkes, how slow
This old Moon wanes; She lingers my desires
Like to a Step-dame, or a Dowager,
Long withering out a yong mans reuennew.

Hip. Foure daies wil quickly steep thēselues in nights
Foure nights wil quickly dreame away the time:
And then the Moone, like to a siluer bow,
Now bent in heauen, shal behold the night
Of our solemnities.

The. Go *Philostrate*,
Stirre vp the Athenian youth to merriments,
Awake the pert and nimble spirit of mirth,
Turne melancholy forth to Funerals:
The pale companion is not for our pompe,
Hippolita, I woo'd thee with my sword,
And wonne thy loue, doing thee iniuries:
But I will wed thee in another key,
With pompe, with triumph, and with reuelling.

*Enter Egeus and his daughter Hermia, Lysander,
and Demetrius.*

Ege. Happy be *Theseus*, our renowned Duke.
The. Thanks good *Egeus*: what's the news with thee?
Ege. Full of vexation, come I, with complaint
Against my childe, my daughter Hermia.
Stand forth Demetrius.
My Noble Lord,
This man hath my consent to marrie her.
Stand forth Lysander.
And my gracious Duke,
This man hath bewitch'd the bosome of my childe:
Thou, thou *Lysander*, thou hast giuen her rimes,
And interchang'd loue-tokens with my childe:
Thou hast by Moone-light at her window sung,
With faining voice, verses of faining loue,
And stolne the impression of her fantasie,
With bracelets of thy haire, rings, gawdes, conceits,
Knackes, trifles, Nose-gaies, sweet meats (messengers
Of strong preuailment in vnhardned youth)

With cunning hast thou filch'd my daughters heart,
Turn'd her obedience (which is due to me)
To stubborne harshnesse. And my gracious Duke,
Be it so she will not heere before your Grace,
Consent to marrie with *Demetrius*,
I beg the ancient priuiledge of Athens;
As she is mine, I may dispose of her;
Which shall be either to this Gentleman,
Or to her death, according to our Law,
Immediately prouided in that case.

The. What say you Hermia? be aduis'd faire Maide,
To you your Father should be as a God;
One that compos'd your beauties; yea and one
To whom you are but as a forme in waxe
By him imprinted: and within his power,
To leaue the figure, or disfigure it:
Demetrius is a worthy Gentleman.

Her. So is *Lysander*.
The. In himselfe he is.
But in this kinde, wanting your fathers voyce,
The other must be held the worthier.

Her. I would my father look'd but with my eyes.
The. Rather your eies must with his iudgment looke.
Her. I do entreat your Grace to pardon me.
I know not by what power I am made bold,
Nor how it may concerne my modestie
In such a presence heere to pleade my thoughts:
But I beseech your Grace, that I may know
The worst that may befall me in this case,
If I refuse to wed *Demetrius*.

The. Either to dye the death, or to abiure
For euer the society of men.
Therefore faire Hermia question your desires,
Know of your youth, examine well your blood,
Whether (if you yeeld not to your fathers choice)
You can endure the liuerie of a Nunne,
For aye to be in shady Cloister mew'd,
To liue a barren sister all your life,
Chanting faint hymnes to the cold fruitlesse Moone,
Thrice blessed they that master so their blood,
To vndergo such maiden pilgrimage,
But earthlier happie is the Rose distill'd,
Then that which withering on the virgin thorne,
Growes, liues, and dies, in single blessednesse.

N   Her.

dett-Coutts library which was dispersed by sale a few years ago. Mr. Walter Spencer, the London book-seller, tells us in his book, *Forty Years in My Bookshop,* that in 1923 a very mediocre copy of the first folio sold in London for fifty-four hundred pounds and a much finer copy sold for eighty-six hundred pounds, or something over forty thousand dollars. I do not know what the record price is at this time but, no doubt, a much higher figure would be realized if a fine copy came on the market today. As time goes on, the price will continue to go higher and higher.

Where are the known copies of the first folio, is a very natural question. A few years ago the British Museum had four, the New York Public Library also had four, the famous J. Pierpont Morgan Library contained three copies, and there were a few single copies in some of the other great libraries in this country.

A wealthy New Yorker, Mr. Henry Clay Folger, some years ago began buying up nearly every good copy of the first folio that came into the market, until he had eight or ten of them in his possession. However, he did not confine his purchases to first folios, by any means, but bought books, manuscripts and objects of art relating to the great dramatist so that after a period of forty years, he had assembled a collection of things pertaining to Shakespeare that was unequaled.

I remember that before Mr. Folger's death in 1930 there was a great deal of speculation as to what would eventually become of this magnificent library and whether the numerous first folios might not be distributed among the great college libraries of the country. Happily, what did happen was this: Mr. Folger bequeathed the library and the entire collection, with an endowment for its maintenance and growth, to the Trustees of Amherst College, who are to administer it perpetually. The library is now housed in a beautiful marble structure, built at a cost of over two million dollars, by the trustees, in Washington, D. C. This simple and dignified building is one of that splendid group comprised of the Capitol, the Library of Congress and the new Supreme

173

Court building. It has a classical exterior and an Elizabethan interior. The exhibition gallery and the theater are open to the general public, while scholars have access to any of the other material in which they may be especially interested. In the gallery are exhibited extensive examples of the wonderful material represented in the collection, including many fine portraits. The theater is interesting as a reconstruction of an Elizabethan playhouse, and occasionally plays are given there with the settings just as they would have been in Shakespeare's time.

Quite recently the library has been extended by the acquisition of the Harmsworth collection, which was, in itself, one of the great English private libraries and especially rich in Elizabethan literature, so that now the Folger Library ranks with the British Museum, the Bodleian and the Huntington libraries as a repository of English books printed between 1475 and 1640.

It is fine to know that through the generosity of men of great wealth, like Mr. Folger and many others, cultural treasures such as these are being made available to the American public.

The year of the tercentenary an incomplete copy of the first folio turned up in London. A dealer offered it to his trade in separate complete plays. Among the four plays offered for sale was one of my favorites, *A Midsummer-Night's Dream,* and I was fortunate enough to acquire it. It consists of the title page and twenty-eight others which make up the complete play. The printing and the paper do not compare in beauty and workmanship to the Gutenberg Bible, produced almost two hundred years before Shakespeare's first folio was printed, but it gives one a fair idea of the appearance of the whole work.

And so Shakespeare did come to America after all, not in person, perhaps, but certainly in spirit! If he were alive today what a harvest he would reap from the sale of his works, the acting of his plays, and, most important of all, the moving picture rights!

The Bard of Avon would then surely die a rich man and, mayhap, leave his wife something more than the "second best bed."

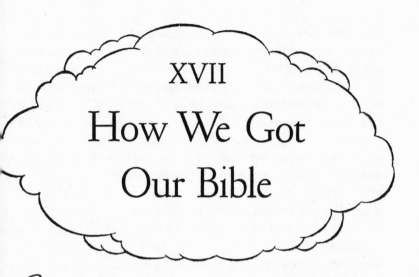

XVII
How We Got Our Bible

$\mathcal{E}$VER SINCE I was a small boy I have wondered in a vague way about the source of the material that makes up our Bible. Where did it come from? And how authentic is it? But I have never chanced to hear anyone discourse on this subject in a way that made any impression on me. I can remember that as a child my earliest impression was that the Bible had been written by God Almighty, revised by Moses, and greatly enlarged and again revised by Jesus. I do not want to seem flippant, irreligious or irreverent in making this statement. Far from it. But no one ever took the trouble to tell me in simple language just how we acquired this, our greatest work of literature, and it was not until a few years ago, when I was privileged to hold in my hands one of the great source manuscripts of the Gothic Bible, *The Codex Argenteus,* that it was brought home to me just how real and how authentic are these great foundation stones that have come down to us from their writers in the early centuries following the beginning of the Christian era.

When one stops to consider how these manuscripts including the Old Testament have survived over a period of three thousand years, how they or the teachings that inspired them came through the centuries of Roman paganism and the following centuries of the dark ages, when the Catholic monasteries were the only islands of learning in a vast sea of ignorance, one begins to realize what a great debt we owe to those saints and soothsayers, scribes and monks, revisers and priests who carried on this great work and gave us the greatest piece of literature we have today. No other book has so long endured, and no other book has been so widely printed as the Bible. A few years ago the statement was made that the American Bible Society alone had printed twenty-five million Bibles and more than one hundred million copies of the New Testament. A noted authority says, "The Bible exceeds in circulation, if circulation may be judged from publication, the next ten most popular books put together. Complete Bibles have been published in one hundred and thirty-five languages, and the New Testament in over one hundred additional languages."

The Old Testament was written beginning probably as far back as the tenth century B. C. The New Testament, according to best authority, was written for the first time during the first century A. D., the Gospel of Matthew between the years sixty and seventy, Mark between sixty-seven and seventy, Luke between sixty and seventy, while St. John was not written until eighty to ninety-five A. D.

Of all the original manuscripts of the Bible no fragment remains today. From what then do we authenticate our Bible? From copies of the originals dating back to the early Christian centuries which were miraculously preserved and which have been discovered from time to time through the ages. These fragments were put together and compared, and each new discovery helped substantiate those that had already been known to exist. There are a few of the early manuscripts written in the Hebrew, but most of them are written in Greek, over fifteen hundred of them being now in existence to our certain knowledge, for the most part in libraries.

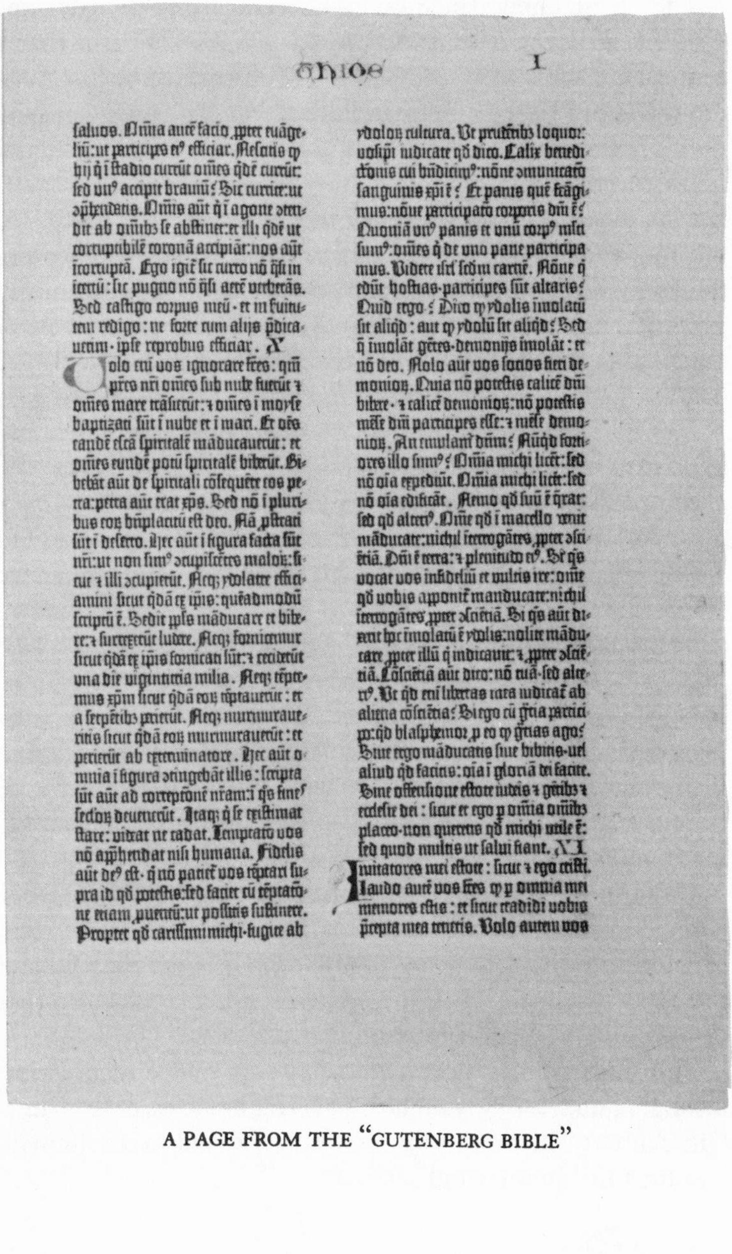

Chios I

saluos. Omnia autē facio ꝓpter euāge-
liū: ut particeps eius efficiar. Nescitis q
hij q̄ i stadio currūt omnes q̄dē currūt:
sed unus accipit brauiū? Sic currite: ut
cōprehendatis. Omnis aūt q̄ i agone cōten-
dit ab omnibȝ se abstinet: et illi q̄dē ut
corruptibilē coronā accipiāt: nos aūt
icorruptā. Ego igitur sic curro nō q̄si in
icertū: sic pugno nō q̄si aerē verberās.
Sed castigo corpus meū · et in servitu-
tem redigo: ne forte cum alijs p̄dica-
verim · ipse reprobus efficiar. X
Nolo enī vos ignorare frēs: qm
patres nr̄i omnes sub nube fuerūt et
omnes mare trāsierūt: et omnes i moyse
baptizati sūt i nube et i mari. Et oēs
eandē escā spiritalē māducauerūt: et
omnes eundē potū spiritalē biberūt. Bi-
bebāt aūt de spiritali cōsequēte eos petra: petra aūt erat xp̄s. Sed nō i pluri-
bus eorū bn̄placitū est deo. Nā ꝓstrati
sūt i deserto. Hec aūt i figura facta sūt
nr̄i: ut non simus cōcupiscētes maloꝝ: sicut et illi cōcupierūt. Neq; ydolatre effici-
amini sicut q̄dā ex ipsis: quēadmodū
scriptū ē. Sedit p̄ls māducare et bibere: et surrexerūt ludere. Neq; fornicemur
sicut q̄dā ex ipis fornicati sūt: et ceciderūt
una die viginti tria milia. Neq; tēpte-
mus xp̄m sicut q̄dā eoꝝ tēptauerūt: et
a serpētibȝ perierūt. Neq; murmuraue-
ritis sicut q̄dā eoꝝ murmurauerūt: et
perierūt ab exterminatore. Hec aūt o-
mnia i figura cōtingebāt illis: scripta
sūt aūt ad correptionē nr̄am: i quos fines
seculoꝝ devenerūt. Itaq; q̄ se existimat
stare: videat ne cadat. Temptatio vos
nō apprehēdat nisi humana. Fidelis
aūt deus est · q̄ nō patiet vos tēptari su-
pra id q̄d potestis: sed faciet cū tēptatio-
ne etiam puentū: ut possitis sustinere.
Propter q̄d carissimi michi · fugite ab
ydoloꝝ cultura. Ut prudentibȝ loquor:
vos ipi iudicate q̄d dico. Calix benedi-
ctionis cui bñdicimus: nōne cōmunicatio
sanguinis xp̄i ē? Et panis quē frāgi-
mus: nōne participatio corporis dn̄i ē?
Quoniā unus panis et unū corpus multi
sumus: omnes q̄ de uno pane participa-
mus. Videte isrl̄ scd̄m carnē. Nōne q̄
edūt hostias · participes sūt altaris?
Quid ergo? Dico q ydolis imolatū
sit aliq̄d: aut q ydolū sit aliq̄d? Sed
q̄ imolāt gētes · demonijs imolāt: et
nō deo. Nolo aūt vos socios fieri demonioꝝ. Non potestis calicē dn̄i
bibere · et calicē demonioꝝ: nō potestis
mēse dn̄i participes esse: et mēse demonioꝝ. An emulamur dn̄m? Nūqd forti-
ores illo sumus? Omnia michi licet: sed
nō oīa expediūt. Omnia michi licet: sed
nō oīa edificāt. Nemo q̄d suū ē q̄rat:
sed q̄d alterius. Omne q̄d i macello venit
māducate: nichil interrogātes ꝓpter cōsci-
etiā. Dn̄i ē terra: et plenitudo eius. Si quis
vocat vos infideliū et vultis ire: omne
q̄d vobis apponitur manducate: nichil
interrogātes ꝓpter cōsciētiā. Si q̄s aūt di-
xerit hoc imolatū ē ydolis: nolite māducare ꝓpter illū q̄ indicauit: et ꝓpter cōsciētiā. Cōsciētiā aūt dico: nō tuā · sed alterius. Ut q̄d eni libertas mea iudicatur ab
aliena cōsciētia? Si ergo cū grā partici-
po: q̄d blasphemor ꝓ eo q gr̄as ago?
Sive ergo māducatis sive bibitis · vel
aliud q̄d facitis: oīa i gloriā dei facite.
Sine offensione estote iudeis et gētibȝ et
ecclesie dei: sicut et ego ꝑ omnia omībȝ
placeo · non querens q̄d michi utile ē:
sed quod multis ut salvi fiant. XI
Imitatores mei estote: sicut et ego xp̄i.
Laudo autē vos frēs q ꝑ omnia mei
memores estis: et sicut tradidi vobis
p̄cepta mea tenetis. Volo autem vos

A PAGE FROM THE "GUTENBERG BIBLE"

The oldest known manuscript in existence is probably the *Codex Sinaiticus* which, it is estimated, was written in the fourth century A. D. This great Codex was only discovered for the modern world in 1844, by a German Biblical scholar named Tischendorf. He spent a lifetime hunting for Biblical manuscripts, and his discovery of this great one in the old monastery of St. Catherine on the slopes of Mount Sinai, and his rescue of it just as the old monks were using the sacred vellum leaves for lighting tapers, is one of the most exciting and romantic stories in bibliographical history. This great manuscript contains the whole of the New Testament, with the Greek text of the Epistle of Barnabas, much of which was hitherto unknown, and the greater part of the Old Testament, all parts of the very manuscript which had so long been sought. Tischendorf had been financed by the Czar of Russia, and so in appreciation of his sponsor, the *Codex Sinaiticus* went to the Imperial Library of St. Petersburg, but was sold in 1933 by the U. S. S. R. to the British Museum, where it may now be seen.

Next following in importance is the *Codex Vaticanus* which may even antedate *Sinaiticus* in antiquity. This manuscript be-belonged to the Church of Rome, was carried off to Paris by Napoleon during the wars, but finally returned to the Vatican in 1815, where it now rests. It contains seven hundred leaves of the finest vellum, is about a foot square, each page containing three columns.

Third in importance is perhaps the *Alexandrian Codex* discovered in 1625. This manuscript comprises seven hundred and seventy-three sheets of goatskin and contains both the Old and the New Testaments. It is the property of that great repository of learning, the British Museum.

Thus we have the three greatest Biblical source manuscripts belonging until recently to the three great branches of the Christian church: The first to the Greek, the second to the Roman, and the third to the Anglican.

During the summer of 1929 while in Sweden, I journeyed to the old university town of Upsala, and there in that interesting library I was privileged to examine one of the great manuscripts of the Bible, known as the *Codex Argenteus*. This famous manuscript is so named because the writing is in silver lettering on a purple stained vellum, with gold capitals. This Bible is the version of Ulfilas, a Gothic Bishop who died in Constantinople in 382 A. D. and is the oldest literary monument in the German language. What a thrill if for only a moment to be allowed to hold this Biblical source material in one's hands!

There are two noteworthy Biblical manuscripts in this country, both in the Smithsonian Institute. The *Codex Washingtoniensis*, containing the Gospels in Greek written in the fourth or fifth century A.D., and sometimes known as the Freer Manuscript. The other is a fragment containing the text of the Minor Prophets written on papyrus. Certain authorities claim this manuscript was written in 270 A. D., and if this is a fact, it is the oldest extant Biblical manuscript.

Between the middle and the end of the second century, the entire Bible was translated by unknown persons into Latin, partly for the benefit of the Roman Church, which at the time was more Greek than Latin, and partly to make the Scriptures intelligible to the Latin speaking church of Southern Europe. The Latin translation of the Old Testament was from the Septuagint. The New Testament, on the other hand, was translated from the original Greek.

During the closing years of the fourth century a scholar appeared whose works made a profound impression on the Bible. St. Jerome, one of the greatest scholars and saints of his time, was asked by Damascus, Bishop of Rome, to revise the existing Latin versions of the Bible. In 385 A. D. his revision of the New Testament was completed, and the Old Testament was afterward translated from the original Hebrew — a task no other Christian scholar of his day could have done.

In speaking of this first great revision of the Bible, Edward Newton says: "It is a great book, the Vulgate, a wonderful book: the production of a monk, who fifteen hundred years ago, exchanging the luxury and learning of Rome for the barren seclusion of a cell at Bethlehem in Palestine, carried through, practically unaided, a translation and revision of the Hebrew Scriptures and with the help of Greek and Latin manuscripts of the New Testament produced a book which for more than a thousand years reigned supreme and unchallenged throughout western Europe. The monk, whom the world calls Saint Jerome, served it well; the most learned man of his age, his work has been called 'the pride and pillar of the Latin Church,' and a great Anglican scholar says, 'It is to Saint Jerome that Europe stands forever indebted for the preservation of her spiritual and intellectual inheritance from the blind deluge of Northern barbarism.' "

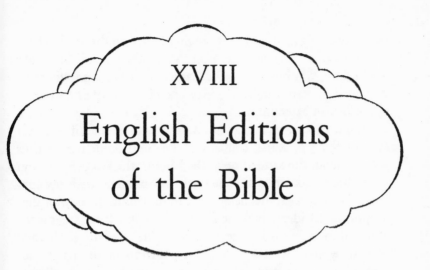

XVIII

English Editions of the Bible

*L*ET US NOW give a thought to what was going on in the early centuries in the land of our mother tongue. Long before the Conqueror came to the shores of Britain and when the world was shrouded in darkest ignorance, the Anglo-Saxon monks were devoting their lives to producing illuminated manuscripts of the Bible. And such illustrations in color, design and workmanship the world has never seen before nor since!

The Lindisfarne Gospels is perhaps the greatest of these and is the earliest English version of the Bible. It is considered the finest example of medieval scriptural illumination in existence. These Gospels were written about 685 A. D. in the old monastery on historic Lindisfarne Island off the bleak coast of Northumberland, so well described in Scott's *Marmion*. The story goes that when the heathen Danes invaded the island, an attempt was made to save the Gospels by shipping them to the mainland. But a storm arose and the vessel rolled so badly that "the Gospels, adorned with gold and precious stones, fell overboard and sank into the depths of the sea." But the monks prayed so earnestly for its recovery that the tide went out as never before and left

181

the manuscript in all its beauty high and dry on the sand. After this miraculous recovery the book, sometimes called the *Book of Durham,* was brought to the Cathedral at Durham where it remained for centuries. It is today one of the greatest treasures of the British Museum.

Almost equally well known and certainly as beautiful is the famous *Book of Kells,* containing the four Gospels in Latin, written about the same time as the Lindisfarne Gospels, but by the Celtic monks in a monastery in Ireland. The Irish say the book was written at the dictation of the angels in the days of the Virgin, St. Bridget, but then you know the Irish are much addicted to fairy stories and romance. The *Book of Kells* also had many narrow escapes from destruction in surviving the raids of the Danes and the Norsemen, but today it may still be seen in all of its marvelous beauty in the library of Dublin University, and is considered by many to be the most beautiful book in the world.

Almost from the very beginning illustration and design have been present in the Biblical manuscripts. In fact art and literature have seemingly gone hand in hand even before the days of the invention of printing, and the great artists for fifteen hundred years have always taken a special interest in portraying Biblical scenes and Biblical characters.

As the western world began to emerge from the deep ignorance of the dark ages, there came a great urge from the masses outside the monasteries to know more about the Bible than the priests and monks were willing to tell them. This desire led to the writing of many more manuscripts — the making of Block Books as exemplified in the *Biblia Pauperum* or Poor Man's Bible, and finally to the invention of printing. It was through this, the greatest invention of all time, that the veil of ignorance was lifted and the layman for the first time in history was enabled to read and study his Bible from his own copy and the exclusive monastic control of Bible teaching was ended forever.

It is not strange that Johann Gutenberg, the inventor of printing, chose the Latin or Vulgate Bible for the first important book to be printed from movable types. The civilized world really demanded it, and in so doing he started a "New Deal," to use a popular expression, to be quickly followed by many other fifteenth century printers in making the Good Book available to the multitudes. The Gutenberg Bible was printed about 1455, and after 500 years is still considered not only one of the first but also one of the finest pieces of printing to come from the hand of man, which towers like a monolith, commemorating that great art to which modern civilization's cultural history owes so much.

As has been said, the old Biblical manuscripts were written in Greek and Hebrew and later in the Latin language of the Church of Rome. With the invention of printing, the Bible became available in German, French and Italian and finally in Spanish and other languages.

Following Gutenberg's issue, many other great Bibles were printed during the last half of the fifteenth century. To mention a few: the Fust and Schoeffer Bible printed in 1462, (these men were the successors to the Gutenberg press); the Bamberg Bible, no copy of which is in America today; the Mentelin Bible, the first to be printed in any modern tongue, German; and the Cologne Bible, which is today even rarer than the Gutenberg.

John Wycliffe was probably the first to translate the Latin Bible into English and give us the so-called Wycliffe Bible, but this translation is apparently rather nebulous and existed only in manuscript until 1840.

The real acknowledged Father of the English Bible was William Tyndale, and here we come at last to a printed English Bible. Never in the history of the church was the clergy more corrupt and contented than early in the sixteenth century when Tyndale was a young man. He had a great ambition to translate the Bible into English and applied to the Bishop of London for

PAGE OF AN EARLY FRENCH ILLUMINATED MISSAL

its authorization. This was denied him by this bigoted ecclesiastic, and it was then he made his famous declaration, "If God spare my life, ere many years I will cause a boy that driveth a plow to know more of the Scripture than thou dost." He was as good as his word, and although driven from country to country, finally in the little German city of Worms in 1534 Tyndale's New Testament was printed for the first time in English, and although thousands of copies were probably made, only three mutilated ones are in existence today. Tyndale, as you know, was hounded the balance of his life by the church, and finally put to death in Antwerp by the intolerant bigots of the time.

The first complete Bible in the English language was the work of Miles Coverdale which he completed at Zurich in 1535. This was in the time of Henry VIII, and the book was dedicated to him. Henry at that time was in rather bad repute with his subjects on account of his marital escapades, and it was suggested by his Chancellor, Thomas Cromwell, and Archbishop Cranmer that it might be good politics for him to sponsor a revision of the Bible. Consequently Coverdale was engaged for the work and produced what is improperly called the Cranmer Bible, or the "Great Bible." This Bible has an elaborate frontispiece by Hans Holbein, and is today a rare book.

In the reign of "Bloody" Queen Mary a small group of protestant exiles fled to Switzerland to escape persecution, and it was there that the famous Geneva Bible was printed in 1560. This Bible was afterward dedicated to Queen Elizabeth when she came into power and reestablished Protestantism. The Geneva Bible is sometimes called the Breeches Bible and will later be referred to again.

During the sixteenth century a number of odd Bibles appeared. There was the MURDERERS BIBLE — where, in the Epistle of Jude, verse sixteen, the word "murderers" is used for "murmurers," the sentence reading, "There are murderers, complainers, walking after their own lusts," etc.

The Bug Bible — Psalm five, "So that thou shalt not nede to be afraid of any bugges by nighte nor the arrow that flyeth by day." Another passage peculiar to this Bible is Peter's exhortation to wives urging them to be chaste and good in which he says: "and if she be not obedient and helpful unto him, endeavoreth to beat the fear of God into her head, that thereby she may be compelled to learn her duty and do it."

The Treacle Bible, in which the text "Is there no Balm in Gilead" becomes "Is there no treacle."

The Breeches Bible, printed at Geneva in 1560, was for years the household Bible of the English race. The seventh verse, third chapter of Genesis reads "Made themselves breeches" instead of "aprons." It was the Bible of the Reformation, of Calvin and Knox and their followers. It was the first Bible that was cut up into verses which could readily be committed to memory.

The Wicked Bible, which leaves out the word "not" from certain of the Commandments.

The Vinegar Bible — 1717 was full of errors. The parable of the Vineyard became the parable of the "Vinegar."

The list of names of men who lived in the sixteenth century whose work had a profound influence on our Bible is a long one. Among them there are Martin Luther, Erasmus, Servetus, John Calvin, and a host of others.

Some years ago as I stood before the large bronze doors which now supplant the old wooden ones of Martin Luther's church in Wittenberg, I was thrilled to think that on this very spot he nailed his bulls against indulgences, which gave impetus to the wave of reformation that was to sweep over the world, and it was from this church that he gave to the world his version, in a German translation of the Bible, which was to be a dominant force in religion in all Christendom.

And now we come to one of the greatest accomplishments in the history of our language: the so-called King James Version of the Bible.

186

Shortly after the death of Queen Elizabeth in 1603, King James of Scotland came to the English throne. James was a scholarly fellow and felt the need of a newly edited Bible to be made under the royal patronage of the King. Accordingly, almost immediately after his succession he called a conference at Hampton Court for this purpose, and there it was decided to make a new translation, and the greatest scholars of all England were called upon to do it.

No more propitious time could have been chosen. The Renaissance was in full flower and such men as Shakespeare, Bacon, Ben Johnson, Beaumont and Fletcher, and many others were all at work on the glorious thing we call English literature.

Fifty-four men were originally engaged in this monumental task. They were divided into six groups, two groups to work at Oxford, two groups at Cambridge, and two at Westminster. As soon as one group had finished a portion of its allotted task, a transcript of the work was sent to each of the other five groups for criticism. In this way the knowledge of all was placed at the disposal of each, co-operation was secured, and an evenness of tone maintained throughout.

These groups of scholars labored thus for four years, and in the end produced the greatest Bible of the English-speaking world, and I believe Macaulay had in mind the King James Version when he said: "The English Bible — a book which if everything else in our language should perish would alone suffice to show the whole extent of its beauty and power."

There were two editions of the Authorized Version in 1611, known as the "He" and "She" Bibles. The distinction comes from a variant reading in the Book of Ruth. The first version read "He went into the city," while the second insisted that "She went into the city." The Great "He" Bible is of course much scarcer and more valuable than the Great "She."

The King James Version was printed in 1611, and marked a new epoch in Bible history. It is the universally accepted and

S. AMPWITTEAHAE

Woiketon 1. 14. Maichcku kuhkomont fonumuh, kah tagunhhamoomoonk pupiffi, wutramhkqwean wutramhkqwean matta howan amoonunk, kah menuhkheunk ufhenaie, netarippe miffinninuog mara woh matcbenehequvog Gotoh qut wurche upu pnubtatramoonganuo peantamwefeon. Ioh wai wefhkeromp wuttattog kommoouk, fg-kefif, fun mara Manittoonoo noh woh faft-marawhont? Sun mara Chepiohhomok-qunoo urtoh woh adr enkappanaut? Neit rohwaj marchefit? Noowtu nuppeantam GOD woi aioquontameh, kah mue nut-ainfhoinntram, qut noh matra paubhranu-mauoo CHRIST. Neumuaue Sampwe-fuaen en romanoch marchefu qut nompaut, kah wanonighae wuffampoowonuah en Sodur, newaj nnanauan GOD woh aioquontamun-aih, noh menuhketeau ummatchefeouk nafh-ge nppeantamoonk, newaj panbahuneg nppeantamoonk, kah matta CHRIST.

6. Rebin. 6 Krhkinneufaonk. Ne qunsf uaiqfwaf mag uuswofhnnwontamut g nppeantamoo. gamo. Howan paioo fhanit Chriftut piyau wequai-yeanr, kah ne wequai wunnaihpe euramuh puppifhppuk ne mara naumaoghay orgonuars, howan moochekebrunk wequai, kah pomnu-tarmoonk ur Chriftur noh moochene naum ummatchefeae penhkenumoon; Paul aiquam quinnuppe.konpauuk panbahtanramup wu tin-naumurus, peantamwefeongafh, neit umnania. Buy nuppemanram; Uppeantamwefeongafh, oghq.

---

oggue putroghamoooaih wunaepagvaih pad-tahguhhamoomoouk pupiffi, wutramhkqwean marchefeonk, neit kuminaue pearram, kah ne wunnaihpe, wahheau webe kuwnkum kummatchefeongfh, kuppeantamwefeongafh kah matta nafhpe JESUS CHRIST.

2. Wame kuppeantam wefeongafh matta woh koowadchanukoob, kah ne nuppoh-guttum yeu/b nafhpe.

1. wanegafh kuppeantamwefeongafh kenk-fuaifh matchefeonk. Newaj fiihamtog GOD, no paich umkwhofurt nafhpe wunfampweufic-onk CHRIST. Ifai. 6. 6. Wame nup-peaniamwefeonganun oggwyeneenikpood ut anaquabii GOD ahpaiquhfunaue mattoengk no pifeh CHRIST uppahketeaunare, kah uppuuttogkommarae nafhpe wunfampwe-feonk. Nifinoh Chriftiaenin nawhurcheyeuoo GOD, Nafhuant, kah nawhurcheyeuoo weyaus.

2. oteh

recognized Bible of the English speaking world, and has been in use for over three hundred years. The influence of this book upon the world has been simply enormous.

Time changes all things, and as the centuries go by undoubtedly there will continue to be new versions of the Bible to conform to the changing interpretation of thought, but the committee that prepared the standard revised version which appeared in 1881, although they made many changes, felt that they were on the whole attempting to "paint the lily" in revising the King James Version.

When the Puritans landed on our bleak New England shores, they brought their Bibles with them as their most precious possessions. These God-fearing ancestors of ours were strong for the Good Book. But the Bible must in those days perforce be printed in the fatherland, as England did not permit her colonies to print Bibles. That was her racket along with taxing tea and other things that brought on the Revolution.

However, John Eliot, a minister who spent a lifetime among the Indians of Massachusetts, brought out the Eliot Indian Bible in 1663, written entirely in the Indian language. This was the first Bible to be printed in this country, and is one of the scarcest books of Americana.

The second Bible to appear in this country was what is known as the Saur Bible, printed in German at Germantown, Pennsylvania, in 1763. It was the first Bible produced in America for civilized worship.

During the Revolutionary War Bibles were a scarce article, but towards its close Robert Aitkin, a Scotsman, a bookseller and publisher, determined to print one and asked Congress for permission to do so. It was his idea that the new government present a copy to every soldier as he was mustered out of the service. Washington was much pleased with the idea, but Congress debated and debated the matter, and meanwhile the soldiers, anxious to get home, disbanded, and nothing was done.

189

However, Aitkin persisted, and in 1782 the work was completed and the first Bible to be printed in English in America appeared. This book is known as the Bible of the Revolution, and only twenty-five copies of it are known to exist today.

The first Bible to be printed in Kansas was a translation of the New Testament into the Ottawa language by that pioneer Kansas printer, Jotham Meeker, on the Shawnee Baptist Mission Press in the year 1841.

This is by no means an exhaustive effort to treat the subject at hand. I have attempted to bring out only a few of the high spots which have contributed to the making up of the Bible as we know it today. There are many famous manuscripts, translations and revisions of the Bible which have not even been mentioned, all important in the contribution they have made to our present day Bible. And so I shall close by bringing this article, covering briefly so many hundreds of years, right down to date by mentioning two recent revisions.

A few years ago our own Doctor Charles M. Sheldon of Kansas brought out an abridged Old and New Testament which he called an Everyday Bible. In this monumental work he successfully attempts a modern version of the Bible by leaving out much of the uninteresting dead wood of the Old Testament, and gives the gist of the Bible, in the Bible language, without comment. The story is told in history and biography, in drama and poetry, in such a way as to make it most interesting and understandable to the average layman. No Christian home should be without a copy of this wonderful compilation of the Book of Books.

And now comes the very latest revision of the Bible. Hitler has employed German churchmen to rewrite the whole New Testament to fit the Nazi scheme of things, and when they have finished tearing it to pieces, the King James version will be an entirely different book. All references to Moses and the Hebrew prophets have been deleted from the New German Christian Bible, and the Book of Books will be made to conform to Nazi theories. Think of this occurring in the homeland of the reformation! What next! Will every country, eventually, have its own version of the Bible, written so as not to conflict with the personal political views of its dictator?

That the Bible *is* the greatest book in the world no one will question. But one seeking an argument will ask, "What Bible do you mean?" To which a noted bibliophile replies, "Any of them." And in the words of the young curate to his astonished congregation, "If the King James Version was good enough for Saint Paul, it is good enough for me."

XIX

Concerning First Editions

ONE COLD WINTER NIGHT, a small group of men, all book-
ishly inclined, were gathered around a great open fire-place in
my library and as the wood crackled and the sparks flew upward,
the subject of our conversation turned to first editions, and finally
one man remarked, in a rather deprecatory tone: "A mere fad,
a passing fancy."

As one who had been indulging in first editions for some
years and grown to appreciate the joy they give a collector, I
resented the remark as being no more justified than saying,
"Christianity! A fad of a couple of thousand years, a short period
of time in history, and known to comparatively few of the
world's population. It will soon pass."

This business of collecting old and rare books is nothing new.
There were collectors, very much like the modern ones, in the
days of the Roman Empire. These men prided themselves, not
so much on the number of their books as on their beauty and
fine condition. Here is a bit of verse by a book collector of Roman
times, evidently written by a rich man who bought books which
his scholar friends would like themselves, but could not afford.

But yet I have them in great reverence
And honour, saving them from filth and ordure,
By often brushing and much diligence
Full goodly bound, in pleasant coverture,
Of damask, satin or else velvet pure,
I keep them sure, fearing they should be lost
For in them is the cunning wherein I me bost
But if it fortune that any learned men
Within my house fall to disputation
I draw the curtains to show my books them
That they of my cunning should make probation;
I keep not to fall in altercation;
And while they commune, my books I turn and wind,
For all is in THEM and nothing in my mind.

A few years ago, a young Englishman, who had made the highest ascent of that King of Mountains, Mt. Everest, lectured in this country on the attempts and failures of this perilous climb. A great many people asked the question, "What good does it do to risk one's life in such a dangerous undertaking? There is no gold, nor precious stones to be found on the top of the mountain; no newly discovered land to benefit mankind, so what good does it do to stand on the roof of the world?"

This same thought is, no doubt, applied to the collector of first editions; what good is it, to possess a copy of a first edition of the book of some favorite author when there are, perhaps, thousands of better copies to be had for much less money?

If one has never been an adventurer in book collecting and has never learned to crave the possession of something that few others are privileged to have and enjoy for his very own, it is hard for him to understand the collector's viewpoint. In other words, you must be inoculated with the germ before you can know, first hand, what the effect is.

As A. Edward Newton, the famous bibliophile says, "The possession of rare books is a delight best understood by the owners of them. They are not called upon to explain. The gentle will understand and the savage may be disregarded. It is the scholar whose sword is usually brandished against collectors; and I would not have him think that in addition to our being ignorant of our books we are speculators in them also. Let him remember that we have our uses."

The other day I came across a cartoon, or an alleged funny picture, representing a man and his guest in a large private library with well filled shelves, reaching to the very top of the room. In a corner of the room is a small book case with one lonely volume in it. "How's that?" says the host, waving a proprietary arm towards the rows on rows, "Every one of them a priceless first edition."

"What's this all alone over here?" asks the guest.

"That? Oh, that's the one I've read!"

Now I wonder if my friends think I am quite that bad when they look upon the rows and rows of books on my library shelves. As a matter of fact, when one acquires a rather large library, not all of the books are meant to be read, by any means. A large number of them are necessarily reference books and used semi-occasionally. Then if one goes in for art books, association books, manuscripts, examples of fine bindings, incunabula and the like, of course, they are not all intended to be read but to be admired purely from an artistic and sentimental standpoint.

But to return to first editions. It was Charles Lamb who stutteringly suggested, "First editions are scarce; tenth editions are scarcer, but there is no demand for them. Why then first editions?"

"The question is usually dodged," says Newton, "the truth may as well be stated. There is a joy in mere ownership. It may be silly, or it may be selfish but it is a joy akin to that of possessing land, which seems to need no defense."

If one is going in for the collection of first editions the question naturally arises as to how and where to start. To begin blindly, without any knowledge of what constitutes a first edi-

But no thing wiste she of his entent
Natheles it happid or they thens went
Be cause that he was her neigheboure
And was a man of worship and honour
And hadde knowen hym of tymes yore
They fallen in speche and so more and more
In to his purpos drew Aurilius
And whan he sawh his tyme he said thus
Madame quod he by god that this world made
So that I wiste I mighte your herte glade
I wolde that day that your Arueragus
Went ouer the se that I Aurelius
Had gone there I sholde neuer come ageyn
For wel I woot my seruise is in veyn
My guerdom is but brestyng of myn herte
Madame rewe on my peynes smerte
Here at your feet god wolde I were begraue
For as wisly as god my soule saue
I ne haue as now no more leyser to seye
Haue mercy swete or ye wol do me deye
She gan to loke vp on this Aurelius
Is this your wil quod she and say ye thus
Neuer yet quod she wist I what ye ment
Ne neuer vnderstode I your entent
By that god that yaf me soule and lif
Ne shal I neuer be vntrewe wif
In word ne in werk as fer as I haue wyt
I wil be his to whom I am knyt
Take this for fynal answer as of me

PAGE FROM WILLIAM CAXTON'S PRINTING OF
CHAUCER'S "CANTERBURY TALES"

tion of some given book, would be the height of foolishness and no doubt, result disasterously. One should, at the very outset, buy a handbook on first editions and have it "handy" before starting in this very intricate game.

Of course, the rarity of a first edition stimulates the desire to possess it. There are few of us who have no taste for rarities.

In no department of collecting is special knowledge so much required as in that of the first edition. The opportunities for mistakes are abundant. No rules can be given; study and experience are requisites for success and, even then, mistakes are easily made.

I was first bitten by the bug in an ideal but accidental way; the way all collectors dream about. I discovered a rare lot of first editions in an old garret, books that had been lying there forgotten for many years. But all the old garrets seem to be getting pretty well cleaned out now, and such luck happens only once in a lifetime.

It was my start, my inoculation, and it set me to wondering what to do next. So I went to a friend, who was a wise old owl, and whose knowledge and opinion on rare books I respected above all others, and asked him what to buy.

"Start with one of the great corner stones of American literature and you can't go wrong," he said. "Pick up a good copy of the first edition of Hawthorne's *The Scarlet Letter* in its original binding while it is still comparatively cheap. It is really one of the great American novels and is sure to increase in price as the years go by."

Some months later when I told him I had succeeded in purchasing a good copy of this book for forty dollars, he exclaimed over the high price I had paid but ended by saying, "Never mind, hold on to it; some day it will be worth what you paid for it."

The first edition of *The Scarlet Letter* has had a great fluctuation in price in recent years but in 1935 it was quoted at seven hundred and fifty dollars and at one time commanded as high as twelve hundred and fifty dollars! How I have longed to tell

A CHAINED BOOK OF THE FIFTEENTH CENTURY

this incident to the man who, at the fireside that night, "pooh-poohed" my childish pastime.

A short time ago, I picked up a copy of *Mr. Sponge's Sporting Tour* with the beautiful hand-colored plates by John Leech, in that most interesting place, the Caledonian market in London. The book has no date but the dealer assured me that it was a first edition. Of course, it proved to be the comparatively cheap second edition but I had paid only a dollar for it, so, at that, I had obtained a bargain and we were neither of us fooled and both were satisfied.

Outside of the dealer in books, I hold no brief for those who collect first editions, or any editions, merely for their possible enhancement in value, but if one must look at it from this standpoint, there is much to be said if one knows his "onions." At the close of the World War, a German friend of mine was the possessor of a large collection of early manuscripts and Incunabula, or fifteenth century printed books. Most wealthy Germans had their fortunes wiped out by the inflation following the war. Not so with my bookish friend. He shipped his books to this country and some years later sold them to the United States government for a million and a half dollars. They are, today, your books and my books, safely housed in the Library of Congress, and were bought at a great bargain.

If inflation should come to this country, the owners of good first editions and other valuable rare books would have a perfect "hedge" against it, for certainly under such conditions prices would be enhanced immeasurably.

I have noticed that most men like to tell of their successes, but forget to mention their failures, and I am afraid all book collectors are especially prone to recount their lucky experiences.

The realm of books is so large and the caprices of man's fancy so varied that no one knows which of the first editions is going to be in demand in the future. That is what makes the game so interesting and so lasting. If this were not so, it would be only

198

a rich man's game or a wise man's game. As it is, one man's guess is almost as good as another's, and that which is cheap and within the reach of the average collector's pocket-book today may have increased many fold in value by tomorrow.

The fact that such men as Dr. A. S. W. Rosenbach, B. P. Widener, Henry C. Folger, J. P. Morgan, Henry E. Huntington and men of much smaller means have paid huge prices for certain first editions, is pretty good evidence that this delightful hobby is not a mere fad. These men knew that the rare first editions of the past, were being rapidly absorbed into the great public and private libraries of the world. They also knew that the number of book collectors was rapidly increasing; and that while the wealth of America was also increasing, the purchasing power of money was decreasing. This all goes to indicate that we may expect to see the value or at least the price of first editions of the really great books eventually go still higher.

Let us not jump to the conclusion from the foregoing that the pursuit of the first edition is a hopeless one for the person of small means. A beautiful copy of the Gutenberg Bible on vellum, the first edition of the first book ever printed, sold a few years ago for three hundred and five thousand dollars. That is one extreme. The other is the secondhand dealer's five-cent box. Between them lies every book in creation. Many of the classics are still within the reach of the most modest purse and if you buy your first edition because it is a favorite book of yours, in many cases it may still be had at almost the publication price. For instance, one might prefer to own, in the first edition, Mark Twain's *The Prince and the Pauper* in preference to *Tom Sawyer*. *The Prince* could be bought for fifteen dollars or less while *Tom* sells for around one thousand. Another even more striking variation of the price in books by the same author is evidenced by the fact that Hawthorne's first book, *Fanshawe, A Tale,* has sold for five thousand dollars while the much better known *Marble Faun* may be had for twenty dollars.

199

Most of us have the idea that age is a determining factor in the value of books, or in other words that the older the book, the greater its value. This is entirely erroneous. There are many books of the fifteenth century that command small prices today while certain volumes brought out only a decade ago are, not only valuable now, but may grow more so with each passing year. Most of the first editions of Joseph Conrad, for example, are now bringing very high prices. A first edition of A. A. Milne's *When We were Very Young,* printed a few years ago, is already more precious than some old tome five hundred years old, totally lacking in human interest.

New books are being born every day, and it is wise to buy them in the first edition, at the published price, if one thinks there is the possibility of their being desirable items in the future. To have bought a copy of the first edition of *Anthony Adverse* would have been more profitable than putting the money into almost any other form of investment. Every old collector has had the experience of making a rare "find" sometime in his career and the book so acquired, at a fraction of its real or ultimate worth, has brought him far more joy than if he had gone out and paid the market price for it; so that, after all, to have made a personal discovery brings the greatest satisfaction.

I wonder if any one could be so totally devoid of literary and artistic sentiment as not to feel a difference between the first edition of the *Canterbury Tales* just as it came from the press of William Caxton, and the ordinary trade edition of today. Could any one fail to be thrilled in handling Dickens' first edition of *Pickwick* with the Seymour and Buss plates, which did not appear in succeeding editions; or to reverence, above all others, the dear little first edition, now so rare, of the *Christmas Carol,* with its hand-colored plates? This by the way was the first and last attempt to so illustrate Dickens.

How many times the first edition of a well known work differs, materially, from later editions. The first edition of Hamlet (1603) is very far from being the play as we now know it. It has only 2,143 lines as against 3,719 lines in the second edition. It is on the second edition, together with the first folio edition that the acting version of the play of today is based.

The story of the first edition of Walt Whitman's *Leaves of Grass* is an interesting one. In spite of the fact that complimentary copies of it were sent to all the leading magazines and newspapers, this edition of one thousand copies would not sell and the books were mostly lost, given away or destroyed. Not discouraged by the failure of the first edition Whitman, at once, proceeded with the publication of a second edition. Emerson had received a free copy of the first publication and had written Whitman, "I greet you at the beginning of a great career." Whitman, who had a keen sense for advertising values, seized upon this for a slogan and printed ∶ in gold letters across the back of the second edition. In the meantime, the public had condemned the work as being "filth," "muck," "obscenity," and "nonsense," so that when the second edition appeared the "Sage of Concord" was somewhat disconcerted, to say the least.

Whitman himself set the type for the first edition, which was published in Brooklyn in 1855. Its long lines and broad margins gave it a dignity not approached in any subsequent issue. The second edition was fat and clumsy but with the Emerson approval printed on the cover and several pages of press notices — most of them, it is believed, written by the poet himself — it sold much more readily than the first edition.

Some books in their first edition are much finer than in any of the succeeding editions. For example: Cadell published in London in 1830, Rogers' *Poems* and *Italy,* containing many beautiful steel plates after Turner. These are two of the most beautiful books in existence, and in the first edition with unspotted plates, they have an increasing value which all lovers of engraving recognize. This is further emphasized by the fact that fine steel engraving is rapidly becoming one of the lost arts.

It has always been one of the anomalies of book-hunting that the original editions of Scott's novels seemed unsought and little valued, while the novels of Dickens and Thackeray brought good prices and were eagerly bought up. The novels of Scott made no stir in the market, but recently a strange thing occurred. It has been found that the *Waverley* first edition 1814, is excessively scarce. As a result, an artificial value has been put upon the few copies that have been in the market, a fine copy selling recently for one hundred and seventy-five pounds, while an equally choice copy of *Ivanhoe* (1820) brought only three pounds. None, but a very rich man, would care to buy a hundred and seventy-five pounds' worth of *Waverley*. How did this book acquire such a value? It is only a fair specimen of Scotch printing upon good clear paper, and bound in the conventional cloth cases of the book-sellers. When Scott began to publish his novels, he was uncertain how he would succeed. *Waverley,* an experimental work, appeared in an edition considerably smaller than that of the other stories. The book was a success from the beginning. It was much read; copies were borrowed, passed about and lost. Many of these earlier volumes of *Waverley* have entirely disappeared. Following this immediate popularity, came a fresh issue in 1814, but the first original issue of the same year grew scarcer and scarcer, until today it is almost never seen. Frankly, it has its market value simply for its rarity caused by the circumstances attending its publication. It contains no matter not in the later editions; the same preface and the same text are there. It adds in no way to our knowledge of Scott. Now, some wealthy book-hunters are willing to pay good money in order that they may own a book which few others in the world are able to possess.

The most remarkable parallel instance on record is that of one of the volumes of Poe. In 1827 Edgar Allen Poe published, in Boston, a tiny volume of poems, bearing the title, *Tamerlane and Other Poems*. The author was unknown at the time, and as a result, the volume was accorded little attention. Indeed, the book was quite forgotten in the early form in which it had appeared. A few years ago, a Boston bookseller unearthed one of these forgotten volumes and it sold in New York for the unprecedented and quite absurd price of nineteen hundred and sixty dollars. It would be hard to say what a *Tamerlane* would bring today, if a copy were to be put on the market, but the book is now listed at ten thousand dollars by some authorities. This is BIBLIOMANIA, indeed, book-hunting run stark mad. The great price is due, largely, to the fact that there is a Poe cult. This has brought book-collecting to the highest pitch of absurdity to which book-lovers have ever gone in their desire to possess unique volumes. This little insignificant volume is a mere curiosity. Its value is for the sole reason that it is the first book Poe published when he was struggling to attain a place in literature. The book itself has no literary value. The poems do not belong to Poe's best period, nor do they mark an epoch in his career. The exorbitant price at which the book is held seems a ridiculous mockery to anyone who tries to attach true value to books as objects of beauty, literary worth or historical value. It is more like dealing in curios than in books.

Let me give one further instance. In 1810 a tiny volume appeared in London called *Original Poetry*, by Victor and Cazire (Percy and Elizabeth Shelley). The price was three shillings and six pence, or about one dollar. Fourteen hundred and eighty copies of the book were printed but only one hundred circulated, the rest being destroyed by Shelley. The book became so rare that its very existence was doubted until Dr. Garnett of the British Museum discovered a copy in 1860. Only two other copies are now known to exist. The book contains seventeen poems which occupy sixty pages and four more pages are devoted to the title page and table of contents. As poetry, the volume is worthless; but it is the first work of the greatest name in the history of English poetry. In November 1903, a copy of this volume sold in London at Sotheby's auction rooms for six hundred pounds, one of the highest prices yet given publicly for any work of an author of the last century.

Of all the modern authors, most of the "firsts" of Joseph Conrad have had the greatest vogue and the most phenomenal rise in price. Whether this is indicative of a lasting appreciation and final estimate of Conrad's ability as a writer remains to be seen. The writer purchased a copy of the first edition of *The Arrow of Gold* at a local bookstore when the book was first published, in 1919 at a dollar and a half. Today it sells at many times that price. It is interesting to know that Conrad made the grammatical error of "absolute strangers" on page fifteen which he caught and corrected in subsequent issues.

Therein lies the whole charm and fascination of the first edition. It is the experimental volume, subjected to vicissitudes and tribulations; the one on which the whole work will succeed or fail. It is the edition which the author has first known and cared for; the first form of the book which later has become famous and made a name for the author. There is an emotional value and a sentimental value in the book just as it comes fresh from the author's pen which will never be equaled in any of the following editions, no matter how successful the book may become nor how many editions it may finally run into. A certain author says, in prefacing his second edition, "They are adding this and they are putting in that, and they have also removed a few 'birthmarks' which gave the first edition the distinction, in Horace Walpole's phrase of being, 'the work of a gentleman, rather than of a professional author.' "

In the foregoing pages, I have made no attempt to discuss the practical or technical side of collecting first editions but rather to emphasize the sentimental side. I have said very little of the factor of condition, the mechanics of collecting or the pursuit of the "point." If one thinks only of the dollars and cents in collecting, he should forget it or become a dealer. A man who considers books primarily as investments or speculations is not a collector. He is in the book business. Now the book business is an honorable calling but a book dealer is not, as a rule, a book collector; he is at the very opposite pole. On the other hand, if one once develops the emotional or sentimental sense for this gentle pastime, a great satisfaction awaits him which will last throughout his whole life and in the end he can join feelingly with Thoreau in saying:

> *I have been a great adventurer*
> *I have discovered Concord.*